FURTHER REFLECTIONS ON
Hazelden's Spiritual Odyssey

FURTHER REFLECTIONS ON

50th
1949-1999
HAZELDEN

Hazelden's Spiritual Odyssey

DAMIAN McELRATH, PH.D.

with a Foreword by

CAROL PINE,
Chair, Hazelden Foundation Board of Directors

HAZELDEN
HP
PITTMAN
Archives
Press

HAZELDEN®

INFORMATION & EDUCATIONAL SERVICES

Hazelden
Center City, Minnesota 55012-0176
1-800-328-9000
1-651-257-1331 (Fax)
www.hazelden.org

Library of Congress Cataloging-in-Publication Data

McElrath, Damian.
    Further reflections on Hazelden's spiritual odyssey / Damian McElrath.
        p.   cm.
    Sequel to: Hazelden, a spiritual odyssey.
    Includes bibliographical references (p.   ) and index.
    ISBN 1-56838-308-8
    1. Hazelden Foundation—History.   2. Alcoholics—Rehabilitation—
Minnesota—History.   3. Alcoholics Anonymous.   I. Hazelden Foundation.
II. Title.
    HV5278.M34   1998
    362.29'86—dc21   98-35227
                                                                    CIP

03 02 01 00 99 5 4 3 2 1

PHOTO CREDITS: p. xiv (Pat Butler Drive); p. 2 (patient life on the units—models, not
actual patients, shown in photo); p. 18 (Clare Harris Room—models shown in photo);
p. 20 (Jellinek building); p. 21 (one-on-one counseling—models, not actual counselor and
patient, shown in photo); p. 26 (exercise room, Cork Fitness Center); p. 33 (interior of
Richmond Walker building); p. 35 (Hazelden's best-selling books); p. 36 (entrance to
Cork Center); p. 39 (Butler building); p. 46 (Family Program building); p. 56 (Tiebout
Hall, meditation center, Bigelow Auditorium); p. 106 (Hazelden walking trail); p. 118
(looking toward the Renewal Center); p. 120 (inside the Renewal Center); p. 121
(outside the back of the Renewal Center)– DENNIS BECKER

All other photos are from Hazelden Foundation photo archives. (Photos on p. 89 and 90
show models, not actual patients.)

Cover design by David Spohn
Interior design by Will H. Powers
Typesetting by Stanton Publication Services, Inc.
Special thanks to editor Gretchen Bratvold

Editor's note
The Twelve Steps are reprinted with permission of Alcoholics Anonymous World
Services, Inc. Permission to reprint the Twelve Steps does not mean that AA has
reviewed or approved the contents of this publication, nor that AA agrees with the
views expressed herein. AA is a program of recovery from alcoholism *only*– use of the
Twelve Steps in connection with programs that are patterned after AA, but that address
other problems, or in any other non-AA context, does not imply otherwise.

Contents

To Hazelden employees, past and present,
all of whom are part of the Hazelden experience
and have done so much to bring the
Hazelden message to others. To these employees,
Hazelden owes its everlasting gratitude.

Carol Pine, chair,
Hazelden Foundation Board of Trustees

Foreword
by CAROL PINE

IN CAMBODIA, an ancient statue carved from stone stands as a monument to the power of vision. Its four faces look simultaneously in four directions: One looks forward to the future, a second looks backward to history and tradition, another looks outward to the changing environment, and the fourth looks inward to core values.

This statue serves as a powerful metaphor for any organization in the midst of growth and change—and particularly for Hazelden celebrating its fiftieth year in 1999. Too often organizations—whether for-profit or not-for-profit—focus only on two faces. They look forward, with strategic plans, to identify how they will capitalize on their strengths, anticipate and serve future market needs, and secure their competitive advantage. They look outward to understand their key stakeholders and their marketplace. While these "two faces of the future" are crucial, the other two faces are equally important. Looking backward to understand an organization's history will inform decision-making and future growth. Similarly, looking inward defines the time-honored values that guide growth, practices and decisions that challenge, provoke, excite, and, in some instances, cause pain.

The organization that fails to honor and understand all four faces is seriously handicapped. Hazelden, thanks to the work of Damian McElrath, has the benefit of all four faces. In his first book, *Hazelden: A Spiritual Odyssey,* Damian, who has been associated with Hazelden for twenty years, charted Hazelden's origin from 1949 through 1987. This new book, *Further Reflections on Hazelden's Spiritual Odyssey*, brings the Hazelden story to the present with an honest, balanced, and highly informative account of Hazelden's recent growth: redefining its mission, expanding its geographic reach, and strengthening its purpose during turbulent times of self-assessment, loss, and change.

Even though the Old Lodge, Hazelden's birthplace in Center City, Minnesota, disappeared to accommodate a large campus of multiple buildings designed to serve thousands who come to Hazelden in ever-increasing numbers every year, in the words of Damian, "While some things have changed, nothing has changed."

Although Hazelden has expanded beyond Minnesota to Florida, New York, Texas, Chicago, and the world through Internet links, and Hazelden's extensive publishing network, "while some things have changed, nothing has changed."

Even though Hazelden now serves 9,500 people and their families in one year and sells books, pamphlets, and other educational materials numbering 3.5 million, one core element has not changed: Hazelden is the caring community it set out to be in 1949. Our reach has expanded in geometric proportions and our possibilities are greater than ever before.

Further Reflections shows us the face of the past and the face of Hazelden's core values that serve as the "compass" of this organization. In doing so, Damian McElrath provides the information and perspective we must have to not simply meet—but embrace—the challenges and choices of our next fifty years at Hazelden. Damian does this in a candid, balanced approach that informs, inspires, and makes us want to read on, learn, and consider all that Hazelden can be.

Introduction

WHEN I STARTED COMPOSING the following essays, I envisioned them as a sequel to *Hazelden—A Spiritual Odyssey*, which was a detailed history of Hazelden's first twenty-five years. I soon decided that the upcoming fiftieth anniversary of Hazelden would best be served by writing some reflective historical essays on the continuing spiritual odyssey rather than by sketching a strictly chronological sequel. Why? Because I was not an eyewitness to the first half of Hazelden's history, whereas for most of the last twenty-five years I have been part of it, lived in it, and relished every moment of it.

I do not believe that my objectivity has suffered, but others may interpret the course of events differently. The contents of this small volume, then, might best be described as historical reflections rather than as strict history. Nonetheless, I have related the history of the last twenty-five years in chapters 2 through 5. The last quarter of a century witnessed a rapid growth and a broad expansion of services (1975–1988), a serious contraction of services accompanied by a series of staff reductions and an unsettling discomfort about Hazelden's future (1989–1993), another period of growth (1993–1998), and finally the extension of Hazelden services to nicotine and related illnesses (1998) to assist people both within and beyond the community recovering from chemical dependency.

The years since 1975 have been truly phenomenal. Scattered throughout the four history chapters are insights into some ongoing themes in Hazelden's history, such as the changing patient and staff profiles and the tension between mission and margin, between paternalism and partnership, between the centripetal tendencies of Center City and the independent leanings of the new Hazelden centers outside of Minnesota. Not content with writing merely a sequential history, I have sought to present themes that ebb and flow throughout Hazelden's history, but principally over the last twenty-five years.

 Reflections on . . .
"I'm Not an Island"

When I got to Hazelden, I can remember thinking that it was everyone else who was wrong, not me. I knew I had a problem, but the way I saw it, I wasn't hurting anyone but myself. I was so supported at Hazelden, and that helped me to see where I was wrong in my thinking. Something that I found out very quickly was how I was *hurting others. You see, I had never been one to reach out for help. I always thought I could do everything on my own, that I didn't need anyone else. One of the biggest things Hazelden helped me with, something that I value to this day, is the feeling that I'm not an island, that I can't do it all on my own, and that it's okay for me to ask for help. During my three years of sobriety, this has been the biggest help for me.*

DENISE Mc.

In the first and last chapters I have offered my own reflections. Chapter 1 looks at the challenge of change during this period and how it affected Hazelden's nature as a caring community. The final chapter addresses the nature of the individual's spiritual journey and the role of Hazelden's services, both old and new.

As I began thinking about the book and its outline, it struck me that the closing of the Old Lodge as a treatment unit in the spring of 1977 served as a natural as well as a symbolic division of Hazelden's history. The closing is sketched indelibly in my memory because I was the chaplain at the Old Lodge when it occurred. Thereafter, Hazelden began to take on a different tone, to which the following essays will testify.

In the years immediately preceding that event, in a quiet and unceremonious organizational shuffle, Pat Butler became the chairman of the board and relinquished his title as president of Hazelden to Dan Anderson. Harold Swift became the administrator. This change allowed Anderson to become exclusively engaged in the promotion of Hazelden. As goodwill ambassador, he assisted in fundraising for the Development Office, spoke at alumni occasions, lectured at Rutgers University, and presented at conferences as far away as Moscow, Russia, and Sydney, Australia. Freed from time-consuming and tedious administrative chores, Anderson had the opportunity to preach the gospel according to Hazelden.

Accustomed to paying attention to detail, Swift became the internal man, responsible for maintaining Hazelden's health. Well into the eighties, Swift kept a steady hand on the rudder of the good ship *Hazelden*, which was to know both tranquil and turbulent seas. His presidency (1986–1991) in many ways served as a transitional time to the presidency of Jerry Spicer. Under Spicer, Hazelden expanded to meet first the extended needs of the chemically dependent community and then the needs of those suffering from other addictions and related illnesses.

In 1993, in the middle of a serious downturn, I became the executive vice president of Recovery Services. I told the staff gathered in Bigelow Auditorium that I had accepted the formidable task because Hazelden had long been a sacred place for me. The spiritual transformations that I witnessed within its hallowed walls dwarfed all the experiences that I had seen in my previous ministry. Hazelden possessed a redemptive character that had to be maintained.

Something that will not go unnoticed is that, like the anonymity espoused in AA traditions, these chapters are filled with people who for the most part are anonymous. I have reduced the cataloging of names to a minimum. Indeed, space precluded mentioning all those wonderful people who have been part of the Hazelden experience and who have done so much to bring the Hazelden message to so many people. Moreover, I am too close to the scene to single out individuals for acclaim (they know who they are). What has to be singled out, or rather multiplied out, are all the members of Hazelden's caring community—the board, staff, volunteers, alumni, partners, and friends of Hazelden—who follow that rich tradition of reaching out to those who come to Hazelden seeking to change their lives in positive ways.

Pat Butler Drive—the road leading into Hazelden, considered by many as "the beginning of the journey," or a spiritual odyssey.

FURTHER REFLECTIONS ON
Hazelden's Spiritual Odyssey

Despite all of the changes Hazelden has endured, the essential spirit of the caring community has managed to perpetuate itself. Patient life on the units has changed over the years, but, at the same time, it has remained the same.

1

The Caring Community and the Challenge of Change

 I N *The Idea of a University,* John Henry Newman wrote of the *genius loci* as the tradition of a place, as the "spirit which haunts the home where it has been born and which imbues and forms, more or less, and one by one, each individual who is successively brought under its shadow."

My own prosaic and less inspired view is that Hazelden's genius—the tradition or guardian spirit that pervades Hazelden's birthplace and that inspires individuals who have been brought into the fold—is the value it places on a caring community. Compassion manifests itself in a gracious environment and a staff respectful of each patient's dignity, wise in the subtle ways of the illness, and expert in treating it. The explosive organizational growth that characterized most of the eighties threatened to undermine this core value. As Hazelden services expanded beyond Center City and then beyond the state of Minnesota, a growing feeling of anxiety arose that Hazelden would be unable to preserve the tradition of a caring community—the spirit that fostered a genuine camaraderie among patients, among staff, and between patients and staff. The anxiety extended to Educational Services, as well. Some of the staff feared that the loss of this spirit would erode the confidence between publisher and consumer as the publishing division sought to acquire markets beyond the recovery community and self-help groups. This chapter explores the threats

3

of change, the evolution of staff, and the enduring spirit of a caring community at Hazelden.

Threats of Change

I have described the closing of the Old Lodge as the end of a stage in Hazelden's history. Its passing marked the end of an era characterized by a simple, uncomplicated approach to treatment. The subsequent changes did not fundamentally alter the program or the processes essential to good treatment, that is, education, fellowship, therapeutic engagement, and continuing care. Rather, change derived from two sources: (1) externally, from legislative, licensure, and other requirements and standards, and (2) internally, due to the evolving patient profile, which became more complicated as the years passed.

Some of these changes were self-evident; others were much more subtle. The effect was more work for the clinicians and less time for the patients. The patients increasingly complained that they hardly ever saw their counselors. In the Old Lodge this never would have been a problem, for one-on-ones were never emphasized. Dialogue with peers and peer input were decisive for recovery. But with the building of the new units in 1965 and 1966, and with the introduction of the multidisciplinary staff, Hazelden placed more emphasis on individualized and personalized attention toward the patients. Externally, licensure and other standards began demanding measurement and accountability, which in turn required more paperwork and attention to medical records. It wasn't only Hazelden; the whole health care system suffered under the same oppressive yoke.

Customer service in each division at Hazelden had its own peculiar evolution. Patient care evolved in four stages: (1) the era of simplicity during the fifties, (2) the multidisciplinary era of the sixties, (3) the regulatory period of the seventies, and (4) the complexities of managed care during the eighties and nineties. While each stage built upon the previous one, strengthening the quality of the treatment process, nonetheless, quantitatively the combined weight of all the changes put enormous pressure on clinicians.

ERA OF SIMPLICITY

Both the way services were delivered and the staff who delivered them changed. As the years passed each generation of counselors yearned for the pristine treatment process of the first generation. Who would not? There were no state regulations, no licensure requirements, no standards from the Joint Commission on the Accreditation of Hospitals to be met, no insurance and managed care companies to satisfy, no treatment planning, no quality assurance regulations. Instead of today's lengthy documentation, the medical record was an index card. The patient was required to talk to the other patients, to make his bed, to go to the lectures, and to comport himself as a gentleman. No wonder Lynn Carroll loved his work and became disenchanted fifteen years later with the arrival of Anderson and his psychological cohorts. Carroll felt that the simplicity of the program was being compromised by the posse of professionals that Pat Butler was bringing in from Willmar State Hospital.

MULTIDISCIPLINARY TEAM

In the eyes of others, these interlopers destroyed the simple treatment approach embodied in the Twelve Steps of Alcoholics Anonymous. They rambled on about a multidisciplinary team, gradually took control of the program, and gave it structure by introducing a detox protocol, individual treatment planning, medical records, a group process, one-on-one counseling, and, worst of all, psychological testing. Carroll felt that it wasn't simple or fun anymore. So he and some like-minded disciples departed.

Those who stayed helped the new generation of treatment givers shape the multidisciplinary team, thereby responding to the multifaceted illness now called chemical dependency. With much sweat and toil the multidisciplinary team forged the Minnesota Model. They felt that it was a simple program, and indeed it was, compared with what was to come, if not to what had preceded it. The criteria for being a counselor also were simple: speaking ability and personal recovery.

THE REGULATORY PERIOD

The clinicians of the seventies were soon confronted with pressures that complicated their work: licensures and certification requirements and a plethora of standards. As the decade of the eighties approached, these staff members, too, began to yearn for the days when their work was uncomplicated and their mission clear and simple. They, too, departed, feeling that it wasn't simple or fun anymore. Others younger than they and to whom they had passed on their clinical skills and wisdom replaced them.

During the seventies, Hazelden itself contributed to the problem. Its reputation for excellence—and the ensuing equation with perfection—put a strain on the whole organization. Hazelden's quest for a perfect treatment planning process led it to adopt the business world's mania for management by objectives in the mid-seventies. The adoption of management by objectives was driven in part by a desire to please the Joint Commission on the Accreditation of Hospitals (JCAH). Hazelden management held the clinicians accountable to a unified system and approach that satisfied the JCAH standards. But the standards complicated the clinicians' lives in a most ungainly manner.

Several times a month, counselors would arrive at work anxious to see how their performance had been graded by management. Whether gratified by As, neutralized by Bs, or despondent over Cs, counselors became distracted by the marking system, and some stayed long hours after work to write the perfect plan and obtain the elusive A. Because these marks could affect raises, counselors were tempted to let the medical record and treatment plans become as important as the patient. Thus evolved the tension between treating the patient and treating the medical record. Even more damning was the increasing practice to write treatment plans that replaced references to AA and the first Five Steps with objectives that smacked of a behavioral approach. Using the Big Book during treatment and referrals to AA as the essential part of an aftercare plan got lost in the struggle to create the perfect plan according to the principles of management by objective. Those counselors who balked at the unwholesome practices were reprimanded and letters to that effect were put in their personnel files.

AA was alive but not well at Hazelden. Alumni and the AA community were alarmed at the direction. A turnabout came in 1978, when Harold Swift, the administrator and a strong supporter of AA, hired a new Rehabilitation program director whose goal was to make AA both alive and well at Hazelden. Those clinicians who had stuck with the Big Book and the Twelve Steps were elevated to key positions, and in a very short time the virus was eliminated. Once again it was expected and popular to include AA meetings in after-care plans and readings from the Big Book in treatment plans. Clinicians and supervisors of the units were able to deal with patients free from the control of a management that lacked the necessary intimacy with patients and their needs.

The clinicians of the eighties were a new breed, trained in regulatory and licensure demands, in quality assurance principles and external accountability. They were used to dealing with bureaucracies and a plethora of paperwork. Throughout it all they maintained allegiance to the fundamentals of the treatment process: patient education through the lecture series, the creation of fellowship through sharing and identification, and the basic clinical services of group meetings and one-on-ones. But unlike their predecessors, the multidisciplinary teams of the eighties were confronted with the challenges of managed care.

MANAGED CARE

Managed care, quite simply, is the delivery of health care in an environment where both utilization and price can be influenced and managed directly. The consolidation, health surveillance, and concentration of control and power that managed care exercises has had a serious impact on Hazelden and its treatment services.

Hazelden's relationship with managed care began in the early eighties, when Blue Cross/Blue Shield of Minnesota began to move aggressively to rein in health care costs, particularly in the areas of mental health and chemical dependency. It did this by demanding increasingly larger annual discounts from care providers. One such provider was Hazelden. In 1981 Blue Cross/Blue Shield demanded a 10 percent discount instead of the 3 percent requested in 1980. In 1986 the insurance company announced that it would reimburse only 55 percent of the total cost. Swift responded by withdrawing Hazelden as a provider. It seemed that Blue Cross/Blue Shield's ultimate goal was to eliminate residential care from its services, and other providers would soon discover this to be true.

This insurance company was only one example of a powerful movement to lower the costs in health care. Insurance companies had never been pleased with the State of Minnesota's early seventies mandate that all insurance premiums carry a minimum of twenty-eight days of residential treatment for chemical dependency. (Hazelden had been a partner in the discussions and an advocate of the twenty-eight-day minimum based upon the model's success.) This displeasure partly derived from the fact that at the time of the discussions, treatment centers were completely unregulated. Insurance companies were somewhat mollified with the creation of state licensure standards, and they were more inclined to deal with Hazelden, especially, since its per diem of $50 was far less than hospital costs and much more attractive than the costs of lengthy stays in a psychiatric ward, which still treated some alcoholics.

As the years progressed, the name Hazelden came to be identified with a twenty-eight-day treatment program, when in reality the name ought to have conjured up a whole continuum of imaginative services that emerged at Hazelden and throughout Minnesota over the course of many years. The success of the model derives from three elements:

1. Its goals are abstinence and behavioral change.
2. The program is linked intimately with the Twelve Steps of AA.
3. Its methodology is based upon a multidisciplinary approach to treatment.

Any program that lacks these characteristics is not a Hazelden model. While a standardized length of stay is not essential, the twenty-eight-day residential program has demonstrated success for individuals needing that level of intensive care.

When managed care began demanding larger discounts, it also began tinkering with the concept and practice of the twenty-eight-day treatment model. As such, managed care appeared to be compromising the integrity of a program clinically tested and experientially proven by the passage of years. It took time to overcome a patient's denial, to initiate behavioral changes, and to procure a commitment to a radically altered lifestyle. Besides, shortening the length of stay risked damaging the fundamental principle that healing and recovery occurs with one person talking to another over a cup of coffee in the supportive setting of Hazelden. Clinical staff felt that they and

Two arial photos of Hazelden, one on this page, taken in 1966, and the other on page 10, taken in 1988, clearly show the foundation's architectural growth, a reflection of the growing success of a mission and treatment model that became renowned worldwide. With growth, however, came new challenges, such as the specter of managed care.

not the managed care gatekeepers knew the needs of the patients—forty years of experience and successful outcomes should stand for something.

But there was another issue in those early years of conflict between Hazelden and managed care. Clinicians did not trust themselves to individualize the program and reduce the length of stay. When Minnesota mandated twenty-eight days of insurance coverage, it was viewed as a real blessing for many people who would otherwise not receive treatment. But it could also be viewed as a curse, for it brought about a complacency among those who practiced the Minnesota Model. Treatment plans began to replicate one another around

four weeks of treatment, stifling the creativity that the Minnesota Model had shown up to that point.

Clinicians knew how to add to the program and increase the length of stay; they knew how to add to the program without increasing the length of stay; but they simply did not know how to decrease the length of stay. Participation in the Family Program is a good example of that dilemma and the fixed way of thinking in which the clinicians had entrenched themselves.

Since its inception in 1972 the Family Program had been recognized as an important dimension of the treatment process. One of the elements that contributed to the success of the program was the participation of patients in group sessions held on the family unit. It was an eye-opener for patients to experience vicariously through another patient's family how their unmanageability had terrorized the family. This opportunity to hear the stories of others was an excellent treatment methodology for the patient. But the three days spent there meant that another part of the treatment process had to be sacrificed. Or did it? In most instances it simply meant squeezing it into the already crammed schedule, rather than waiving the Fourth and Fifth Steps until the patient left treatment, or eliminating work on the Second and Third Steps when the social and trust goals of the Family Program could have been a very adequate substitution.

For years supervisors and counselors had succumbed unwittingly to the quantification principle; namely, that more is better. From this point of view, the sacred substance of a twenty-eight-day program becomes a moot issue. For the patient the pace was too hectic and overwhelming. The members of the multidisciplinary team vied with one another for appointments with the patient, and the patients complained that they did not get to see their counselor often enough. In the wake of all of these needed and added services, how could clinicians reduce the program to less than twenty-eight days? Besides, what was to prevent a twenty-eight-day program from being reduced to a twenty-one-day program, and then to fourteen days, and then to seven, and then to a three-day detox program? That scenario had already sounded the death knell for a number of treatment centers.

Who was driving patient care—clinicians or insurance? It was difficult for clinicians to be a caring community when they were focused on insurance demands.

EVOLVING PATIENT PROFILES

Another challenge to the multidisciplinary team of the eighties and nineties was the evolving patient profile. Patient types can be looked at either by demography or by the issues that patients present. In the case of the former, Hazelden did very well in accommodating the needs of men in 1949, of women in 1956, of young people in 1981, and of senior citizens in 1991. Hazelden led the way in applying the term *chemical dependency* to both alcohol and other mood-altering substances and developed a basic treatment model applicable to all.

Hazelden was quick to realize that many patients had multiple issues to deal with. But it was very cautious in its response to issues outside its expertise in chemical dependency. Consequently, if the assessment process discerned emotional, financial, legal, or marital problems, these would be clearly noted, briefly talked about, and then relegated to aftercare planning. But as the profiles of the patients became increasingly complicated, the inadequacy of this approach became more and more apparent to some of the Rehab staff. They felt that if some of these issues were not dealt with in a more timely fashion during treatment, the chances of relapse would increase. As a result, special groups and lectures were conducted, for example, for victims of abuse and for patients who had eating disorders. Psychological services were offered for those patients who had mental or emotional problems.

The Center for Ongoing Recovery was established in Center City in 1995 to respond to the mental and emotional needs of any recovering person. Modeled after the counseling clinic that had been licensed at the Hazelden Center for Youth and Families in 1993, the Center for Ongoing Recovery is a clear example of Hazelden's embrace of a holistic approach to treatment of chemical dependency.

In the early nineties Hazelden began studying patient profiles to map out clinical pathways for various categories. These efforts will help individualize the patient's stay while simplifying clinicians' work. Perhaps clinicians will once again be able to have fun, that is, to find fulfillment in helping people recover, even if the counselor's role is not as simple as it once was.

Central to Hazelden's future is matching the evolving patient profile with staff professionalism and competence. The current alcohol and drug abuse clients will look very different from those patients of one or two decades ago. They will arrive at Hazelden with multiple emotional, mental, and physical problems in addition to multiple drug problems. AIDS will continue to be a crucial factor for many alcoholics and drug patients. Research has projected that 25 percent of clients will be HIV positive. The professional's role will continue to evolve. Hazelden's counselors of the future will have more education, possessing more specialized skills and broader knowledge than the professionals today. They will need to deal with broader mental health issues, and there will likely be pressure to move from the chronic disease model to a mental health one. Physicians, psychiatrists, and psychologists will play a major role in the delivery of Hazelden services, and chemical dependency professionals will need to team up with mental health agencies. Case managers increasingly will have to work more closely with the patient's hometown community services. Vital to Hazelden's caring community concept is its ability to provide more holistic services that meet the needs of the evolving patient profile.

 Reflections on . . .
"The Greatest Gift of My Life"

I'm a completely different person now, and my perspective about who I am is completely different. I was kind of closing down right before I came to Hazelden, and my life had a very narrow focus. I discovered that by letting go of my old life, I allowed so much new to come in. Work, relationships—every part of my life is better.

I used to think I was a very shallow person, particularly when I listened to people talk who'd been in the program for a while. I remember when I first came to treatment, I was asked what awed me, and I couldn't think of anything. Now I can talk about love and service. And I'm awed not just by what's happened, but by how I've changed.

And another thing: I found my belief in God as a result of recovery, and that was something I never sought out or struggled to get to. It just came. Today, it's the greatest gift of my life—something in which I find great strength and peace.

ARIE N.

Evolution of Staff

While the emphasis in the previous pages has been on clinical staff, *all* staff, not just Recovery Services staff, have contributed to the legacy of a caring community. Rather than single out individual staff members for praise, these paragraphs are intended to do justice to the inestimable contributions of generations of workers to make Hazelden a household name.

In 1949 there were four staff members. By 1990 almost a thousand employees worked at the various Hazelden sites. By the late nineties, despite staff reductions earlier in the decade, that figure remained the same. Besides the striking change in numbers over fifty years, a corresponding change can be observed in the profile of employees, who now support a variety of services in a multiplicity of settings. Both numbers and profiles were accompanied by a startling evolution in attitude, or spirit. Numbers, profile, and attitude: All three affected one another and together formed the ingredients of an evolving employee culture that deserves serious recognition in the history of Hazelden.

A statement in the Byrd Report (a 1983 audit of senior management at Hazelden) captured a guiding principle of Hazelden: "We are committed to maintaining the spirit of smallness." Yet the gradual loss of this spirit was probably a fundamental reason for the transformation of the staff culture.

The Rehabilitation Program was settled in Center City primarily because of the manor's tranquil environment. At first the addition of other buildings, particularly in 1965, did not compromise the rehabilitation environment. The setting, together with the smallness of the operation, fostered among all the staff a sense of familiarity, of family, of closeness. The efforts of all were directed toward Hazelden's mission—helping people get well.

It was simple and fun, and all staff could see concrete results deriving directly from their efforts. There were few if any secrets, even after the program added four and eventually six new units. Housekeepers and maintenance people were part of the team. First names and nicknames abounded. No one stood on a title, although the maintenance people were always served first in the dining hall. The AA fellowship's motto of unity and service was deeply embedded and profoundly practiced at Hazelden in the first twenty-five years of its existence. The patients from the extended care unit, Jellinek, worked side-by-side with the mail-order clerks in the basement of Lilly. The fiscal people, the research staff, the training supervisors and trainees—all felt part of a family intimately united by a belief in service to others: helping people change and actually seeing the changes occur.

The sense of compassion was contagious and crossed departmental boundaries. The units, toasty warm in the winter and gloriously sun-filled in the summer, were the centers of a caring community that embraced both patients and staff. The cooks sent down fresh brownies in the morning and the housekeepers made sure that bowls of candy adorned the coffee tables. The spirit of smallness fostered humility. What did that mean? Simply that it was not the talents of the individual staff member that counted most, but the collective power and talents of all the staff. The staff modeled the "we" of the Twelve Steps. The caring community of patients and staff reflected the spiritual awakening of the Twelfth Step: "I cannot do it by myself; I need others to help me." In those early years the entire staff functioned as an informal multidisciplinary team. Not until the late sixties did the professional clinical staff become the formal team.

During the seventies, as the multidisciplinary team refined the Minnesota Model, the clinical staff took great pride in the model's propagation throughout the country. It took awhile for all the disciplines on the team to sort out their roles and assume their places. But gradually the chaplains and the nurses joined the psychologists and the counselors at the staff meetings. Then the recreational and aftercare specialists began to participate in the formulation of the patient's treatment plan. During the seventies the participation was active. The team felt obliged to be at staff meetings; the "we" concept prevailed. When disagreements led to shouting matches with egos and control issues getting in the way, someone eventually had the good sense to refocus everyone's attention on the real issue: "What is best for the patient?"

The implementation of the Minnesota Model gradually changed in the eighties. Some of the change had to do with the loss of the spirit of smallness, some of it had to do with the competition among the disciplines for the patients' time, and much of it had to do with the complexity of the patient profile. As the years progressed, the staff meetings were less and less attended by the various disciplines. Clinicians were spending more time on other responsibilities—paperwork, one-on-ones with patients, and other meetings. The relocation of the Psychology Department to the Cork building separated multidisciplinary teams. Pastoral staff was reduced with the closing of the Clinical Pastoral Education Program in 1992. Some of the counseling staff had difficulties accepting a changing role for counselor trainees. Taken together, these changes had a large impact on the teamwork inherent in the multidisciplinary concept. Without a doubt the ideal was still alive and each discipline contributed to the patient's plan, but the personal input and interaction that once took place at the unit staff meetings no longer existed.

The spirit of smallness was missed by other staff as well. As Hazelden expanded nationally and as the Center City staff multiplied and separate divisions moved into separate buildings, the staff became strangers to one another. The culture became increasingly corporate, which only further stifled the spirit of smallness.

Through a series of climate surveys, senior management tried to discover why this spirit was missing. The staff issues were always the same: lack of communication, lack of teamwork, and unfavorable benefits. From the staff point of view, the response from senior management never seemed adequate. In an attempt to recapture the spirit of smallness, Dan Anderson and Harry Swift hosted a series of weekly lunch meetings with groups of employees. These discussions about Hazelden's history, tradition, and core values continued for a whole year. But it was too late to restore the spirit of smallness. An employee counterculture had emerged and for better or worse was there to stay. Some defined the difference between the two cultures as the difference between mission and margin.

Underlying the tension between mission and margin, between service and business, between the passage from one culture to another was the specter of change that haunted each generation of employees. Change came in different forms, from different sources, and at different speeds. Some employees could handle it; many could not. Those who could not generally became passive.

The Enduring Spirit of a Caring Community

Has the specter of change in the name of progress affected the treatment process and the sense of a caring community that permeates that process? Despite all the changes Hazelden has endured, the essential spirit of the caring community has managed to perpetuate itself. How?

Nostalgia for old customs and traditions never dies. Those rituals that are tested, tried, and true retain a prominent place in our lives. Some others pass away, and still others rise in their place. Patient life on the unit changes but remains the same. The graduates of the units all carry with them reminders, tokens of the pain and the happiness they have experienced. The Old Lodge was torn down in 1988, but its library was transported book by book and shelf by shelf to what used to be the old dining hall, now called the Clare Harris Room.

When the Old Lodge ceased to be used as a rehab unit in 1977 there was much grieving among graduates, some of whom traced their lineage all the way back to 1949. Its halls and rooms had been hallowed by the number of death-rising experiences that had occurred there. The memories of the great and wonderful things that happened in its hall, nooks, and crannies would never be forgotten

The Clare Harris Room

by graduates, including the Golden Slippers (the repeaters) who walked the corridors of the Old Lodge. Some of the lodge's traditions still continue on Cronin. For example, the men on this unit still line up to march together to the dining hall and the lecture hall. While some things have changed, nothing has changed.

The daytime schedules are more structured, but the night unit staff still encounter fraternization in the most unlikely places. Storytelling in both formal and informal groups remains an essential component of treatment. Waiting to tell one's story still creates high anxiety and continues to have startling purgative effects. Cocaine addicts and alcoholics still mingle just as easily over coffee when it comes time to recall and share examples of unmanageability.

The old store, where one could get the bare essentials such as cigarettes and candy and clothing, has now found a new home, called Serenity Corner, in the Cork Center. Alumni can measure Hazelden's growth with a simple visit to Serenity Corner, where every imaginable item now caters not only to patients' needs but also to their whims and wants. Change can also be measured by the increased number of patients that wend their way to Ignatia Hall and its annexes for medications, a clear testimony to the

18

changing patient profiles. The old road under the elms can never be replaced in the memories of those who walked it. But sharing on walks, now on several nature trails, continues to have an important place in the program. While some things have changed, nothing has changed.

The veteran patients on the units continue to do their own brand of Twelfth Step work for the newly admitted, whose anxiety levels are still extraordinarily high despite the bravado fostered by well-entrenched defense mechanisms. But while piercing through the denials of the rookies, the veteran patients take pains to do it in the same nonjudgmental fashion that had been shown to them when they first arrived. These veterans still maintain the cohesiveness of the unit, and their experience still guarantees the validity and honesty of the group conscience. They safeguard Hazelden's reputation for confidentiality: "What is shared here, stays here." While some things have changed, nothing has changed.

Dia Linn and Lilly, the women's units, continue to guard their privacy with a zeal and jealousy that goes back to 1966, when the women were transferred from White Bear Lake to Center City. Graduation ceremonies still reflect the uniqueness of each unit, moving patients to joyful tears and creating lasting friendships. The staff on these two units, now usually all women, have introduced services to deal with abuse and other emotional problems to help ensure ongoing sobriety and serenity when the women leave Hazelden. Visiting Sundays continue to witness sometimes tearful, sometimes angry reunions with parents, sons, daughters, spouses, friends, and lovers. While some things have changed, nothing has changed.

Jellinek increased its capacity from twenty-three to twenty-nine beds, and the staff's understanding and skillful treatment of the patients continues to enhance Jellinek's national reputation. Returning alumni admire the additional landscaping surrounding the extended care unit. Winston Churchill was the name of the basset hound that came from across the lake to visit with the patients on Jellinek. The patients taught it to stand up on its hind legs while the group said the Serenity Prayer. Winston is long gone, but the Serenity Prayer is still recited. While some things have changed, nothing has changed.

The Jellinek building on the Center City campus. Jellinek houses a nationally recognized program for extended care.

The housekeepers are still essential to the multidisciplinary team and report on the completion of the therapeutic tasks and the tidiness of beds and rooms. Returning patients often want to see the housekeeper, whom they remember affectionately while having forgotten the lectures and the names of the people who delivered them. The only thing that the millionaire from Texas wanted to see when he returned for a visit was whether the coffee room was still kept clean, the therapeutic task that meant so much for his recovery. While some things have changed, nothing has changed.

The distinctive flavor of each unit, first reflected in their different names, continues with the diverse approaches of unit supervisors and staff and with the special traditions of each unit. Each unit now has an annual reunion at the Renewal Center where friendships are renewed, stories are shared, hugs are given, and recovery is strengthened. Patients are proud of Hazelden, but they take even greater pride in the unit from which they graduated, whereof they have the fondest of memories. While some things have changed, nothing has changed.

Peer reviews have replaced the hot seats. There are no more

Counselor with patient. By demonstrating regard for the whole person, Hazelden offers a unique, high-quality treatment package in which chemically dependent people receive appropriate care.

statements from the coffee-room balcony and no more therapeutic screamings on the frozen lake, and the neighbors no longer telephone when meeting time is announced over the outside speakers to inquire what is meant by "mating time." But the basic expectations for all patients remain fundamentally the same as they were in 1949—behave yourself, talk to one another, make your bed, and go to the lectures. While some things have changed, nothing has changed.

Hazelden's guardian spirit retains its faith in the value of a caring community. In 1998, as in 1949, Hazelden's units still demonstrate this core value.

In 1994 Rehabilitation Services was renamed Recovery Services. The change reflected the division's concern not just with what occurred at Hazelden in primary treatment but also with the individual's lifelong journey of recovery. Recovery is an integrated journey—a spiritual odyssey requiring continual growth and not a single, static transformation. Hazelden's mission is to instill in the people who seek its help the wisdom that has been entrusted to Recovery Services: Recovery is an unending journey graced by change, growth, and individual dignity and worth.

1955: Old Lodge with initial annex, referred to as Nightmare Alley, that was built from donations given by Pat Butler's father, Emmett Butler. The closing of the Old Lodge as a treatment unit in 1977 marked the end of an era in Hazelden's illustrious history.

2

The Sirens of Success

THE CLOSING OF THE OLD LODGE
as a treatment unit in 1977 marked the end
of a chapter in Hazelden's history. For the
next decade it housed various departments and individual offices until it was torn down, with nothing except a rock to memorialize the
sacred spot. The loss of the Old Lodge did not just symbolize the end
of one era and the beginning of another. In reality much of the creativity, simplicity, personalism, and sense of individual caring associated with the Old Lodge were replaced by more systematic,
institutional, and formal approaches, corporate in structure and
leaning toward the bureaucratic. Although much of this was due to
licensure and accreditation requirements, Hazelden, like other communities that have evolved into institutions, has experienced a loss
of the original inspiration and fervor that made the pristine ideal so
attractive and appealing to those who were initially drawn to it.

The passage of time witnessed many changes in personnel, atti-
tudes, approaches, and emphases. The year 1989, for example, was
remarkably different from the year 1949 when Hazelden first
opened. In 1949 the founding fathers purchased a beautiful country
farmhouse in a serene setting outside Center City, a rural village
with less than three hundred people. Located fifty miles north of the
hustle and bustle of the Twin Cities, that quiet refuge mushroomed
into a large complex of buildings and corporate offices. The Old
Lodge has vanished and the buildings that now share the grounds

with the treatment units have crowds of people streaming in and out of them, infringing upon the solitude and the stillness that enhanced the treatment process.

The changing external environment, with its intrusion upon rehab space and solitude, and the institutionalization of the community are but some of the factors that confirmed and reinforced the advent of a new era. The spirit that guided the early years and inculcated a sense of family was now accompanied and sometimes overshadowed by an equally important business mindset. Strategic planning, corporate goals, and a fiscally sound policy with an annual surplus became necessary if the not-for-profit foundation were to survive and grow. Managed care would challenge the legislated mandated coverage of residential treatment and threaten the very existence of primary treatment. Leadership became corporate and communal and would no longer be linked to individual personalities. Gone were the days of Carroll, Butler, and Anderson.

Characteristic of this new era in Hazelden's history were the growth of Educational Materials and the birth of Professional Training. These two divisions replaced Rehabilitation as the creative spark of Hazelden. Innovation, once Rehabilitation's birthright, would be claimed by Educational Materials. With a revised and expanded mission statement, Educational Materials and Professional Training reached for wider markets and audiences.

Between 1974 and 1998 Hazelden's services expanded at a phenomenal rate, then contracted, and then expanded again. During this period, the board of trustees grappled with Hazelden's mission, senior staff received a stinging rebuke from a management survey, and Hazelden endured a changing of the guard. The contraction of services brought about a painful downsizing—a first in Hazelden's history—which caused great stress and took its toll on staff morale. In spite of, or perhaps because of, these events, Hazelden appeared to have emerged stronger, more disciplined, and more focused in doing what it knows how to do best.

Hazelden's linear history has had its peaks and valleys, its sorrows and joys. But that history has also had its cyclical dimension, a recurring tension between continuity and change, the permanent and the passing. As human beings we experience similar tensions; we fear the unknown. Like human beings, institutions have a life of their own and experience critical junctures or crises. At Hazelden, change beckoned in a number of different ways.

The Byrd Report

In 1983 a highly controversial management audit called the Byrd Report (after the consultant who conducted the survey) was completed. The controversy revolved around three sensitive issues: (1) the succession from Dan Anderson, the president of Hazelden, and the strengths and weaknesses of the principal candidate, Harry Swift; (2) a team culled from middle management (a decision bound to unsettle senior management) conducted the survey; and (3) Hazelden's future was viewed in terms of "orthodox versus unorthodox philosophy."

The part of the report dealing with the presidential succession was so sensitive that this section of the final document was not sent to all board members. Instead, the consultant read from this section at the board meeting. Moreover, the orthodoxy statement led some members of the board to conclude that Hazelden's philosophy of treatment was being compromised. In fact, the Byrd Report raised the issue of orthodoxy not in regard to Hazelden's treatment philosophy but to describe a conflict of goals within the senior management team. It was a conflict over whether to expand Hazelden's services into areas that appeared to be foreign to Hazelden's mission.

The Byrd Report went on to say that in the past the senior management had been philosophically cohesive, although Educational Materials was regarded as more business oriented. The Rehabilitation Division regarded itself not in terms of profit margins but rather in terms of service. The potential expansion of Hazelden into prevention and health promotion, the report continued, raised divisive questions among the senior management directors: "Who is and who is not orthodox? What is orthodoxy now, and what is it to become? Rehabilitation has been the key to Hazelden's success, but the business mix is changing and threatens the philosophical fabric so carefully woven since the beginning of Hazelden." In other words, were areas unrelated to Rehabilitation or even to chemical dependency legitimate avenues of pursuit for Hazelden?

The Struggle to Expand Hazelden's Mission

The questions about orthodoxy led to hot debates about Hazelden's identity and mission. This was not just a philosophical issue; it was a practical one, too. Joan Kroc, the wife of the hugely successful entrepreneur of the McDonald's franchise, had already sent out tenta-

The exercise room in Cork Fitness Center

26

tive feelers to Hazelden about establishing on its campus an educational center for prevention and health promotion and a special rehabilitation unit for professional athletes. The fact that the Kroc Foundation would build and endow the whole facility to the tune of $7 million made the proposal very attractive.

From the beginning, however, there was some disquiet about segregating the athletes from the rest of the patients and then providing them with a special training facility for working out and keeping in shape. Such special attention did not fit the Hazelden model in which everyone was treated as an equal, in which unit assignment was determined by the vacant bed, and in which the treatment program was not sacrificed to any secondary needs, especially recreational in nature. Furthermore, the athlete's competitive nature could be a serious stumbling block to treatment, especially in the acceptance of the First Step. How could a power hitter be powerless?

After a series of discussions the board decided to accept the Kroc Foundation's proposal on two conditions: (1) athletes would not be given special treatment; and (2) the athletic facility could be used by all patients and employees, and athletes would follow the same recreational schedule as other patients. The fitness center was to contain an exercise (Nautilus) room, swimming pool, elevated running track, and courts for basketball, volleyball, and racquetball. Included in the new complex would be ample space for educational and training services, especially in the field of prevention.

Accepting the Kroc proposal signaled Hazelden's serious commitment to prevention and health promotion. Though prevention had been a part of Hazelden's mission before, the field had been entrusted primarily to Educational Materials, which produced educational publications about chemical dependency and its consequences for the individual and the family. But coupled with health promotion, prevention now assumed a broader mantle. According to Dan Anderson, who for years had been the outspoken champion of prevention, Hazelden's future goal was to help people of all ages change their lives in positive ways. The board was being challenged to expand Hazelden's target population from the recovery community to everyone who needed help. But the board did not appreciate nor was it ready for the implications of Anderson's vision.

The mission debate grew increasingly intense in 1984 and reflected three major concerns:

1. Would Hazelden be overextending itself by becoming all things to all people?
2. Was Hazelden able to transfer the technology and skills that it possessed in treating chemical dependency to other addictive behaviors?
3. Was adequately trained staff available to undertake all these endeavors?

After a lengthy and sometimes passionate discussion, the vote on the revised mission statement ended in a tie. The proposal was tabled and staff was asked to further research the concerns that had been raised. In reality, many of the board members did not want to go beyond the traditional mission of treating just the chemically dependent and their families.

Before the next meeting Pat Butler wrote a letter to all the board members in which his customary perspicacity, foresight, and wisdom were readily apparent. In referring to the growth of Hazelden over the past thirty-five years, he noted that the scope of

Dan Anderson, president emeritus of Hazelden and Hazelden's leader, 1961–1986. It was Anderson's and Pat Butler's influence that inspired the Hazelden board to expand the mission statement in 1984 to include services and related support for other addictive behaviors as well as appropriate community services, namely prevention and health promotion.

28

activities had gone far beyond what the founding fathers of Hazelden ever could have imagined. He said that they would have been aghast at the range of activities Hazelden is presently engaged in, and doing them all in such a competent fashion. In looking to the future, Butler noted that Hazelden would have to explore additional opportunities to be of service to people. Hazelden would encounter some strong adversarial forces, such as dramatically increased competition, regulatory constraints, and a decrease in third-party payment.

Butler foresaw that the patient population would become increasingly complex and the leading treatment centers would be expected to respond to multiple addictions as well as emotional and mental health problems. Consequently, it would be wise to consider all options.

In addition, Butler observed, Hazelden should be willing to discuss and explore the applicability of its technology to the treatment of other addictions. "Some of our friends in recovery literally kill themselves with food and tobacco addictions," he wrote. Staff was quite capable of constructing an appropriate peer group model for other addictions were Hazelden to enter those fields. The competition was already doing more than just exploring those potential areas. Butler asked quite poignantly, "Should the 'pioneer' be lagging behind?"

 Reflections on . . .
"I Don't Think You Have to Be an Alcoholic or Addict to Learn from the Twelve Steps."

I'm a registered nurse, and as a nurse coming into the program, I assumed that Hazelden could help me fix my mind and body. But I found out that that wasn't really enough. From a spirituality standpoint, given the abusive stuff I'd grown up with, I had given up on any kind of God or Higher Power. My time at Hazelden certainly brought back the feeling that it's okay to have a Higher Power, that you need to have somebody to help you through the rough times. Being

*introduced to the Twelve Steps was so good for me. They're
a way of living, and I don't think you have to be an alcoholic
or addict to use and learn from them.*

DENISE Mc.

Moreover, he felt strongly that Hazelden should consider the potential application of the Twelve Steps and the self-help model to other chronic illnesses. He thought highly of the staff: "We have a good competent staff with an outstanding track record that does not include much precipitous behavior. In fact, I think they are even on the somewhat conservative side of business. . . . You can count on them to look into these problems without in any way jeopardizing the effectiveness of our existing programs."

Butler enjoyed the challenge of change as he wrote, "In summary, I think we should keep our options open—all of them."

At the special board meeting on August 9, 1984, Dan Anderson gave a presentation of the history of change at Hazelden and of innovative responses to changing needs. The presentation combined with Butler's letter triggered a long, intense, and open discussion of Hazelden's mission, and eventually these two men inspired the board to expand the mission. According to the new statement, issued in 1984, Hazelden would now provide services and related support for other addictive behaviors as well as appropriate community services, namely, prevention and health promotion.

This revised mission statement became the cornerstone of the expanded and innovative services established in the subsequent years. While the Rehabilitation Division discussed developing new services for other addictive behaviors, only periodic seminars were added for smokers. Despite Butler's exhortation, the division failed to utilize its tested technology in creating residential treatment models for other addictions. Furthermore, it failed to capitalize on the holistic approach that the multidisciplinary team could offer, instead continuing to reserve to aftercare any other problems that might beset chemically dependent patients. Rehabilitation was not ready to change. The sirens of success lulled the division into complacency. It would take another decade before services were introduced to respond to the mental, emotional, physical, social, and spiritual wellness of patients while they were still in treatment.

But if the Rehab Division did not change overnight, Educational Materials was willing and happy to take advantage of the expanded mission statement. Its list of publications multiplied, its revenues soared, and potential audiences for meditation books appeared unlimited. By the mid-eighties, Educational Materials grossed more than 50 percent of Hazelden's revenues, while Rehab fell behind to about 40 percent. The Richmond Walker Center, publishing's new home completed in 1985, was a visible testimony to that growth. The history of Educational Materials is probably the clearest and brightest, but not the only, response to the challenge of change that Hazelden encountered during the period from 1975 to 1990.

History of Educational Materials

When Educational Materials became a separate division in 1975, it began to shape its own character, at first secondary to, then the equal of, and finally independent of its older sibling—Rehabilitation Services.

The first stage in this evolution was sustained by the decision to produce books on alcoholism not just for the Hazelden family but for the whole recovery community. The subsequent decision to distribute AA's World Service Books, which included publications on Al-Anon, required that the division expand beyond its core publications and move aggressively into the market by reaching the shelves of bookstores.

Educational Materials published *Not-God*, the history of Alcoholics Anonymous, in 1979. The production of the "Caring Community" series launched the division into the video field. By the late seventies the growth of Educational Materials was so rapid that it began publishing materials having little to do with chemical dependency. This concerned the board, which directed the division to limit its new publications to those serving the recovery community.

But that retrenchment was short lived. The year 1980 signaled the beginning of a decade that was creative and exceptionally productive. The 1980 publication of *Food for Thought*, which addressed the problem of eating disorders, opened the door to books on other addictions. To those who protested that this was not Hazelden's mission, the response was that recovering people could very easily lapse into eating disorders.

In 1982, two years before the board issued a revised mission for the Hazelden Foundation, Educational Materials drew up its own expanded mission statement, extending its market beyond the recovery community. Two criteria in the revised mission made it acceptable to the board. The division would not publish anything in support of controlled drinking or contrary to the Twelve Steps of AA. Soon after, Harold Swift disbanded the literature advisory committee, which, because of the strong membership from the Rehabilitation Division, had been inhibiting the growth of Educational Materials into other areas. This new freedom to publish books on unexplored subjects guaranteed the division's success and ample profit margins, which allowed Hazelden to support its many building projects and to carry other less profitable or nonrevenue-producing services.

A very visible sign of the division's growth was the expansion of facilities, starting with the extension of the warehouse in the Butler building. Two farmhouses that Hazelden had inherited served as editorial offices, but everyone knew that this space was not adequate. In June 1984 the board authorized building a new facility that would house the division. The Richmond Walker Center was completed the following year. Though it required a very large outlay of money, $3.5 million, by that time the division was accounting for more than half of Hazelden's gross income.

A combination of factors account for the rapid and voluminous growth of Educational Materials in the eighties. The introduction of computerized technology improved customer services. An emphasis on marketing plans and sales departments increased earnings. And a lack of competition allowed Hazelden to occupy a singular place in the literary world of chemical dependency, until others saw how lucrative this market could be.

The real breakthrough, however, came with the publication in 1982 of *Each Day a New Beginning*. While recognizing the singular contribution of *Twenty-Four Hours a Day*, the author of *Each Day* believed that something distinctive and different was needed for women. Some people in Educational Materials and on the literature advisory committee remained skeptical, so much so that twenty-five positive reviews of the manuscript were obtained in an attempt to get the project approved. Finally, Swift's order to go ahead with the book ensured its publication. *Each Day* was an instant and smashing success. The first printing of ten thousand copies was sold out even before it hit the warehouse. Two hundred and fifty thousand copies were sold the first year.

What is just as significant as the volume itself was the fact that it became the model for other meditation books. Recognizing the unmet need for this type of literature, other publishing houses began imitating the product. The expansion of Hazelden's mission and its outreach to more and more people—families and friends of chemically dependent people, adult children of alcoholics and of dysfunctional families, those suffering from eating disorders and

Interior of Richmond Walker building, home of Hazelden Information and Educational Services

other chronic illnesses—was clearly reflected in its publication of meditation books that appealed to a broad range of people. The number of people who could be helped through these publications seemed to be endless. Emboldened by this success, the board gave permission to tap the market overseas. In 1988 a corporation called Hazelden Publishing International was formed with a distribution center in Cork, Ireland, to facilitate the division's move into the international arena.

Rich veins had been discovered in the publishing mines, and Educational Materials was tapping them as fast as it could. As the division produced a continuous stream of innovative literature, Rehabilitation Services grew jealous. The old refrains were sung anew: Were we in the business of making money or the mission of serving people? Of course the two were not incompatible and no one division had an exclusive claim on serving people. Psychologically, the Rehab Division felt as if it had made the better choice because it dealt with the more important subject—real people—while its younger sibling dealt in books. Bibliotherapy could not match individual or group therapy. While Rehab looked backward at past glories and took hubris in its vocation of helping people, Educational Materials looked forward, taking pride in its flexibility and the ever-widening audience that tasted its food for thought.

Scores of new videos and films were produced for which Hazelden won a number of awards. It was a name to be reckoned with. Harper and Row, San Francisco, recognized the audiences that Hazelden had captured and signed a contract with the foundation to distribute selected titles. In 1987 Educational Materials reached the pinnacle of its success when it published a book that made *The New York Times* bestseller list. Written by Melody Beattie, *Codependent No More* probably did more to enhance and spread Hazelden's reputation than any other product. It ensured the division's success for the next several years. But fame had its downside as once again Educational Materials came into conflict with the Rehabilitation Division.

Educational Materials had stuck to its promise not to publish anything not in accord with the Twelve Step program and philosophy. Moreover, the recovery community was still one of its principal target audiences. But with the Beattie book the question of orthodoxy once again raised its serpentine head, and the two siblings looked at one another with suspicion and mistrust. On the one hand, the Rehab Division did not consider codependency an illness and refused to diagnose it as such. On the other hand, a stream of books flowing from Educational Materials maintained codependency was an illness, and the leaders of the codependency field felt betrayed by the Rehab Division at Hazelden. Both friends and foes were wondering what Hazelden's official position was.

The success and fame that came with Beattie's book and subsequent publications would not last forever. Just as had happened earlier in Rehab, the sirens of success were at work in Educational Materials. By 1990 the general population's interest in recovery had peaked and was beginning to wane. Educational Materials had succeeded because the content was good and its staff knew where the market was going. But that market had become saturated. For the

Three of Hazelden's all-time best-selling books: Twenty-Four Hours a Day, Each Day a New Beginning, *and* Codependent No More

next several years the emphasis shifted from producing new and innovative products to the defensive measures of reducing costs and raising prices. By 1991 Educational Materials' sales were in a steady decline as treatment centers closed and the requests for bibliotherapy rapidly diminished. By 1993 contingency planning had become an accepted part of Hazelden's vocabulary.

Prevention and Health Promotion

Like Educational Materials, the Cork Center, completed in 1985, was another testimony to the innovative powers unleashed and supported by the revised mission statement. Even before that, in 1981, Dan Anderson had directed some of Hazelden's resources to the area of prevention. He encouraged more direct approaches to

Entrance to Cork Center, which became Hazelden's center for training and fitness

36

prevention, one of which would be getting into the educational system of the country, at every level, to educate teachers and students about substance abuse and its consequences. This was a natural outgrowth of the Professionals in Residence Program, initiated in the mid-seventies for the Minnesota Educators Association. Educators from throughout the state came to Hazelden for a week to live and mingle with the patients on one of the rehabilitation units. The venture was so successful it was extended to include other professionals: social workers, nurses, psychologists, administrators, and physicians.

The agreement reached with the Kroc Foundation ensured that prevention would become part of a newly formed division called Health Promotion. The division would encompass a wide variety of programs promoting healthy lifestyles, vocational changes, and prevention. The goal was to teach people of all ages to change their lives in positive ways.

A contract with the National High School Athletic Federation carried the Hazelden message to thousands of students in thirty-two states. Workshops on the implications of chemical use on adolescent sexuality, a central developmental task for adolescents, alarmed the traditionalists at Hazelden, who believed in focusing narrowly on chemical dependency and not on related problems. Some people at Hazelden felt that focusing on prevention would eventually put Hazelden out of business. The ultimate decline of the Health Promotion Division and its closing at the end of the eighties was not because of its message but because of financial constraints and the consequent lack of administrative support. Despite this short duration, the division's widespread impact helped Hazelden attain national prominence in the field of prevention.

While Educational Materials and Health Promotion took the lead in advancing Hazelden's national reputation, other services made significant contributions toward the same end. For example, the employee assistance programs sponsored by Hazelden eventually assisted people with problems other than chemical dependency. A short-lived contract with the National Football League also provided Hazelden and its employee assistance programs with national exposure. Training and educational services were more popular than ever, and the services of the Consultation Department were in great demand.

This national reputation was one of the principal reasons why the Development Office was able to make its case so strongly and so successfully for funds from Hazelden stakeholders. Annual fundraising increased from $1.3 million in 1987 to $4.5 million in 1994. In 1987 the Development Office established an endowment fund, which by 1997 totaled $23 million. Both Pat Butler and Harry Swift believed strongly that fundraising would play an increasingly important role in Hazelden's future. Given the national and innovative thrust of Hazelden's services, it wasn't difficult to convince people that Hazelden had the best product on the market.

Geographic Expansion

Besides the innovative directions mentioned in the previous paragraphs, Hazelden continued to expand its more traditional services by planting them in other geographic areas. Rehabilitation Services, despite its more measured and conservative approach to the new mission statement, had a major role in this expansion. Hazelden's 1981 purchase of New Pioneer House in Plymouth, Minnesota, and its subsequent establishment of two group homes in Wisconsin for adolescents responded to the national need for services for young people. To treat this population demanded a well-trained, experienced, and sensitive staff. This is exactly what Hazelden inherited from Pioneer House. Gradually, the facility became recognized nationally as a center of excellence for the treatment of young people.

Hazelden began expanding to other locations outside of Minnesota. In 1986 the Hanley-Hazelden Center in Florida opened a primary residential treatment program, which over the years developed a full continuum of services. It was soon recognized as a center of excellence for the treatment of senior citizens. In addition, Hazelden New York opened in 1992, and Hazelden Chicago opened in 1997.

Expansion of the Center City Campus

Back on the Center City campus in Minnesota, the construction of buildings continued at a rapid pace. Besides the Cork and Richmond Walker Centers, the Renewal Center and the Nelson Bradley Dining Hall were constructed. The Butler building was renovated and expanded to fulfill expanding administrative needs. The extended care facility, Jellinek Hall, was remodeled to the satisfaction of the patients. All this was financed by the high census in primary treatment and by the gross revenues in Educational Materials. At the same time, staff increased from 222 employees in 1979 to almost 1,000 in 1990.

The front of the Butler building, home of Hazelden's administrative offices

This broad-brush description provides some idea of the amazing growth that occurred in the early and mid-eighties. But a mere recitation of data doesn't quite capture the creative and innovative energy that was present. As we have seen, Educational Materials and Health Promotion took the lead. The revised mission statement allowed these divisions to help people in a variety of ways.

Given the growth and expansion of services, given the national and international reputation, given the financial stability and the support from stakeholders, Hazelden's success and future prosperity seemed guaranteed. But there were blips on the radar screen that harbingered some stormy weather.

Nelson Bradley Dining Hall

Reflections on . . .
"A Challenge, But a Good One"

My sobriety and my work at Hazelden has enabled me to totally rebalance and refocus my life—thankfully! My treatment has enabled me to reignite a lot of friendships and family relationships that had been completely dormant for a number of years—and now my relationships are real. My life has a much more appropriate balance between work, friends, activities, family. I have also been able to reprioritize my life. Now my family has become much more important to me. I've become much more even-keeled and much more considerate of other perspectives on life and other approaches to life. In my day-to-day relationships with others, I think I'm much easier to speak to and much friendlier. This is not to say I'm always that way, of course, but I'm much more like this than ever before in my life.

There are still other things I need to work on too. This newfound balance in my life actually makes it more hectic, more full—and I'm still learning how to handle that. It's a new challenge, but a good one!

MURRAY S.

Harold Swift,
president of Hazelden 1986–1991

3

The Changing of the Guard

MUCH OF THE SUCCESS described in the previous chapter can be attributed to Harold Swift's leadership as administrator and then as president of Hazelden. When he succeeded Dan Anderson as president in 1986, he came to the position well-seasoned by his twenty-year apprenticeship at Hazelden. Pat Butler appointed him administrator in 1976 for his tenacity and skill at paying attention to detail. Swift used the next ten years of his tenure to establish Hazelden on very strong financial footings. He was indefatigable in his efforts on behalf of the treatment field, and as a result of his active participation on national committees, he commanded a great deal of respect from other prominent providers as well as from many outside the field. While he may not have possessed the oratorical gifts of his predecessor, he was just as active on the speaker's circuit and was respected for his knowledge and insights into the strengths and weaknesses of the treatment field and the threats posed to it, especially from managed care.

In some major respects, the Byrd Report provided the raw material and the directives out of which Swift's presidency was molded. In responding to these directives, Swift in many ways served as a transitional figure during a drawn-out changing of the guard from the old multidisciplinary order led by Anderson to the new corporate partnership forged by Jerry Spicer.

The Byrd Report, completed two years before Swift became

president, had concluded that the talented directors of the various divisions were unintentionally creating parochialism at Hazelden. They were not coming to grips with change and its impact on Hazelden's overall mission and philosophy as well as on the direction of each division. Some of the directors were looking to the past for guidance, while others were paying attention to the marketplace. The Byrd Report concluded, "They have not been sharing in a 'big picture' that would permit them to tie their goals into Hazelden's goals. They end up in memo battles, hard feelings, and 'empire building.'" The directors' rebuttal was that if indeed staff increasingly identified with their own division's mission and colleagues and less with the umbrella mission of the whole foundation, then the board was partly to blame for this because it had not provided a clear direction.

The board was surprised and somewhat alarmed by the Byrd Report. While not endorsing everything that appeared in it, they directed Swift to deal with the outstanding issues and resolve them. Writing to Pat Butler shortly after the board's directions, Swift noted, "Since the Byrd Report, they [the division heads] have been gun shy, if not hurt deep down inside." But he did not think that their problems were unique nor anywhere near as serious as one might perceive from reading the Byrd Report. Moreover, he did not believe that the teamwork among the directors was as lacking as the report suggested. However, in accordance with the board's wishes, he would work hard on morale and team building at the top.

While concerned about the damage and hurt feelings caused by the Byrd Report, Swift was also hurt and angered by the report's critique of his own qualifications or lack thereof for the presidency. It was in this context that he wrote to Pat Butler in February 1985: "If the board has any ambivalence about me (as Dan's replacement), they should post the job." He continued quite prophetically that Hazelden would be heading into some rough times in the next four or five years, "and that will occur regardless of who gets the job. Thus, I wouldn't want an ambivalent board added to the list of problems that we will have." His remarks about the board's ambivalence proved remarkably clairvoyant and did prove an added burden as the next five years unfolded.

One of the first tasks that Swift undertook as president was to develop a structure that evolved into the two-tiered administrative organization originally proposed in the Byrd Report. He reduced his span of control to five direct reports. Spicer, his chief operating officer, had five directors reporting to him. Swift's principal purpose was to organize in such a fashion that the directors could engage in interdivisional dialogue necessary for the best interests of all of Hazelden. The structure remained in place until 1993, when Jerry Spicer succeeded Swift and reorganized in a manner consistent with his own vision. Under the direction of an outside consultant, Swift and the directors participated in a very intense seminar to overcome the parochialism among the divisions. The seminar helped them find a common focus for all divisions and cultivate interdivisional communication.

With a new organizational structure in place, the division directors could now engage in the serious business of strategic planning for the state, national, and international growth essential to Hazelden's future. For example, in 1987 the business plan centered on an expansion of regional hubs: Hanley-Hazelden in the Southeast, an alliance with Tufts University in the Northeast, and programs in Dallas-Fort Worth in the Southwest. While goals and directions did change (e.g., Fellowship Club in New York replaced Tufts as the Northeast hub), growth nonetheless supported by solid business plans replaced the grazing strategy that had guided Hazelden in the past. Under Swift, first as administrator and then as president, growth within the parameters of financial stability and the revised mission statement became hallmarks of the eighties.

Warning Signals

Not everything, however, was successful. The failures did not individually detract from the overall success, but considered together they foreshadowed the contraction that was to come. It was difficult to recognize and interpret these omens amid the larger context of success, but they created an undercurrent that added to the charged atmosphere in which Swift took over the helm as president.

THE FAMILY PROGRAM

The Family Program, one of the most important adjuncts of the treatment process, had grown rapidly since its inception in 1972. Growth in numbers demanded more and more space. In 1986 when the educational and training programs moved to the new Cork Center, the Family Program occupied their quarters in the Osborne building. But as insurance companies began refusing reimbursement for the Family Program, the high census it enjoyed in the late seventies and early eighties gradually declined, stabilizing at about 60 percent occupancy in the nineties. Through the decline, Hazelden had steadfastly refused to diagnose as an illness the problems that the family (aside from the chemically dependent) experienced—family members were affected by the illness, but they themselves were not sick. Proponents of codependency were chagrined by this position because their hope for reimbursement depended upon a medical diagnosis acceptable to insurance companies.

Family Program building

46

OUTPATIENT PROGRAMS
AND OTHER PROFESSIONAL SERVICES

Hazelden's track record with its outpatient programs was disappointing. In 1981 it turned over one of its rural programs to the hospital in Cambridge, Minnesota, and in 1986, effected the same transfer in Alexandria, Minnesota. In 1984 it closed its outpatient program in St. Paul, and in the same year decided against managing one in New York. It sustained a measure of success with the women's outpatient program in Minneapolis, at one point expanding it into day and evening sessions. But a subsequent and steady decline in referrals forced the closure of the day program, and then in 1991 the evening program was also shut down. The previous year the outpatient program in Texas also had been closed. The same fate befell the two adolescent group homes in Wisconsin, which were closed in 1986. A lack of referrals, insufficient reimbursement, and staff problems were among the reasons for their demise.

In 1987 Burlington Northern did not renew its contract with Hazelden as its preferred provider of treatment services. This action very soon became part of a larger pattern: Managed care could offer services at a lower cost. Many of the companies with which Hazelden had long-standing relationships began opting to have managed care companies run their employee health care plans.

FALLING REVENUES

In the mid-eighties the board began to emphasize the business side of Hazelden—profit margins and productivity. Many of the board members felt that Hazelden's survival was at stake. The balance between business and service still concerned the board, but as one member, Mike Conley, reminded the others in 1986, "While I think it critically important to remember the spirit of Hazelden's mission, the fact remains there will be precious little service to provide if we don't remain viable as a business. I hope we can keep this always in mind— particularly in the difficult years we'll see ahead for the treatment industry."

In order to consolidate its resources, cut its losses, and safeguard its nonprofit status, Hazelden Services Incorporated was formed in

1988. This served as an umbrella corporation for Hazelden's professional services: Health Promotion, Employee Assistance Services (both of which were losing money), Continuing Education Services, Research and Consultation, and the outpatient programs in Texas and for women in Minneapolis. By 1991 all of these departments had either been sold or shut down except Continuing Education, which was moved to the Educational Services Division. After a lifespan of only five years and renovations that had cost hundreds of thousands of dollars, the Hazelden building on Park Avenue in Minneapolis, which had housed most of these departments, was leased to another organization.

Discouraging news continued to come from a variety of sources. Although the board had been led to believe that Hanley-Hazelden was doing well, it was not reaching its projected census and continued to lose money. In 1991 it showed an operational shortfall of $1 million, which Hazelden absorbed. In 1989 Educational Materials suffered its first budget shortfall, and in 1991 Hazelden's retail bookstore at Har Mar Mall in St. Paul, Minnesota, was closed after only one year of operation. After three years of operation, the distribution center in Ireland was still unable to break even.

Overall, the year 1990 saw flat revenue growth, low census, an overall drop in operating margins, and little success in influencing the marketplace and public opinion despite strong initiatives in both those areas. The gravity of the situation became clear in 1991 when for the first time the census in Center City dropped below budget expectations. To soften the impact on those who read the report, particularly the board members, the news was reported this way: "Although occupancy was below its goal, it was above the national average." Small consolation to those members who were accustomed to Hazelden's traditional waiting list.

 ## *Reflections on . . .*
"A Liberating, Freeing, Enlightening Feeling"

My time at Hazelden helped me learn something else that continues to be very important in my life—to look at what part I play in any given interaction. I still remember when my counselors suggested I look at this. I thought they were so stupid! I said to myself, "Hey! I didn't ask to be abused, I didn't ask for all the stuff that happened to me." Finally, though, I was able to say that yes, bad things happened, but now, what can I do to make things better for myself? This was really important for me. I see that I have a role in all my interactions with others. This understanding has also helped me be able to let go of the things I don't have any control over. I know now that I can't change what happened in the past, but I can change what happens in the future. I can't change the fact that my family is still alcoholic, but I can change how I interact with them. This has been a very liberating, freeing, and enlightening feeling. I know now that I can take care of me.

DENISE MC.

Damage Control

Some board members, nervous and uncomfortable with the stark reality of empty beds, thought that the New York Fellowship project should be delayed, even suspended. They considered the situation grave enough to warrant cutting Center City staff to balance the budget, and Swift was instructed to carry out the downsizing. Swift agonized over this, for he believed that Hazelden staff were more important than the money set aside for marketing and public relations. The so-called voluntary exit program of 1991 was a first for Hazelden. Sixty people lost their jobs. The era of paternalism had come to an end.

In 1964 Lynn Carroll had complained about the amount of money that was being spent on the new buildings instead of increasing staff salaries. In 1991 staff had to pay the price for the excessive expansion of the eighties. The fact that it mirrored a national phenomenon was small consolation to those whose relationship with Hazelden had been severed. Clearly, external forces were at work that threatened the present and the future of Hazelden. Hazelden had survived a critical juncture like this once before: In 1966 many believed that Lynn Carroll's departure signaled Hazelden's demise. At that time, psychologists and counselors struggled for what was thought to be the soul of Hazelden. Now, in the early nineties, the staff reduction seemed to signal Hazelden's demise, and it could be interpreted in hindsight as a foreshadowing of Swift's departure. The changing of the guard from Swift to Spicer had to grapple not only with the soul of Hazelden but also with its financial survival. In this charged atmosphere some saw the events in the backdrop of a struggle once again between mission and margin. But though the two may have seemed incompatible, Hazelden really wasn't selling its soul for thirty pieces of silver.

With great reluctance Swift agreed to intensify marketing and public relations efforts at the expense of staff in 1991. He felt that Hazelden's reputation took care of any need for marketing. He balked at the decision to hire a public relations firm for the same reason. On the other hand, in the arena of public policy, he believed that Hazelden needed to play a prominent role in order to counterbalance what he considered the pernicious influence of managed care.

Managed Care

Swift felt that any attempt to work with managed care would compromise both the high quality of the Hazelden model and the good results that this model produced. He was prescient and tenacious in his belief that managed care would eventually deny benefits for any form of residential care and perhaps even for outpatient services. Many people in the field agreed with him. The subsequent closing of facilities appears to have argued in his favor. On the other hand, many of the more influential board members disagreed, insisting that managed care would remain an integral part of the health care scene. They considered an adversarial role detrimental to Hazelden's future well-being.

By the mid-eighties the insurance companies had managed to bypass mandated coverage by insisting that the patient demonstrate medical necessity. The criteria for medical necessity were determined by the managed care company, which made them so stringent and narrow that only a small percentage could qualify.

In all fairness, managed care did have some legitimate grievances against the chemical dependency treatment providers. In the early eighties, hospital administrators were desperately looking for ways to fill their vacant beds. The insurance-covered chemical dependency industry appeared especially lucrative. At the same time, treatment centers and clinics proliferated and the fierce competition to maintain a high census was exacerbated by unprofessional tactics in filling those beds. Addictions multiplied; anyone rumored to be addicted was a likely candidate for treatment. Some referrals were overdiagnosed or misdiagnosed.

The media highlighted the abuses, shunting aside decades of dedicated service. The insurance industry, chafing under the rash of reduced profits, shed its diapers and donned the boxer shorts of managed care and began cuffing the ears of the mental and chemical health fields, looking for an opportunity to deliver a knockout blow. The treatment field felt the pummeling, and treatment centers began to close at an accelerated pace.

Some traditional professionals in the treatment field lent their own voices to the protestations, proclaiming that treatment was ineffective, that abstinence was unrealistic, inhuman, even un-American, and that the disease concept of alcoholism was the fiction of someone's fertile imagination. In the mid-seventies, the *Rand Report* had noted research about the efficacy of controlled drinking. Now the report was resurrected and the banner of controlled drinking was raised once again, to the satisfaction of those who felt that loss of control was a myth since there wasn't anything that Americans could not do if they set their minds and their wills to it.

Led by managed care, this army marshaled against the chemical dependency field was a formidable foe. Swift convinced the board that a stand had to be taken. His decision not to sign a contract with Blue Cross/Blue Shield in 1986 was a bold but risky one. No one could foresee the consequences. Support for Swift's position gradually eroded. With the retirement of Pat Butler as chairman of the board two years later, some board members began to urge that the president take a more conciliatory tone toward managed care companies.

Growing Internal Friction

It was a difficult time. Painful contraction after years of expansion began to set in with the closing down or selling off of some of Hazelden's operations. Swift was also caught in the riptide created by pressures from the fledgling New York and Florida programs and the business mentality of some of the board members. Another crosscurrent was created by the friction between those board members who placed a high priority on development funds for regional expansion and the old-timers who cautioned against expansion in favor of safeguarding the gains that had been made in Minnesota. The board was undergoing its own metamorphosis. As Hazelden expanded, the newly drafted members from outside Minnesota wanted their voices heard.

The issues of managed care, marketing, public relations, staff downsizing, strained relations with New York, and the apparent failure of Hanley-Hazelden all contributed to a growing friction between the president and concerned members of the board. In addition to staff reductions, these board members insisted on selling off or closing down nonproductive divisions, such as the Employee Assistance Program and Health Promotion. These same board members began taking a more active role in the management of Hazelden, a not-so-subtle way of exhibiting their lack of confidence in the president's leadership. But besides these issues there were other, less obvious factors that found Swift standing alone.

The diminishing roles of Pat Butler (who died in 1990) and Dan Anderson were a serious loss, not only for Hazelden and the whole field of chemical dependency, but for Swift as well. Butler had been the patron of Hazelden for almost forty years, and, together with Anderson, he supplied and nurtured the creative energies that brought Hazelden renown as a pioneer.

When Swift became president he had to fill the shoes of two charismatic people. Indeed, he had to do it at a time when all the gains that had been made in the field of public opinion and public policy were in danger of being lost. It appeared that the educational process begun fifty years ago had come full cycle. Public awareness and belief that chemical dependency was an illness and could be treated was fast losing ground. Likewise, mandated coverage for treatment was no longer a given.

On a more personal note, Swift was Butler's choice for administrator in 1976 as well as for president in 1986. When some board members hesitated in their support of Swift for president, Butler's support overcame their reluctance. He saw Swift as dependable, loyal, and devoted to Hazelden's mission. The relationship between the two was more than just employer-employee; it bordered on friendship. Had Butler intimated a more conciliatory move toward managed care, Swift may well have moved in that direction. On the other hand, perhaps like Lynn Carroll twenty-five years earlier, Swift might have felt that he still could not agree with the direction that the board was taking, in particular the directive to lay off staff in 1991. With Butler's departure and death, Swift lost the individual who had been his greatest supporter over the years. (One keen observer of the events of these years remarked that if Pat Butler had played an active role for another five years, Swift would have survived.)

Beyond Paternalism

Butler's departure also signaled a loss of continuity. Guiding Hazelden from 1952 until 1989, Butler was regarded by board members as the Grand Old Man. No one was willing to question his leadership. Butler's uninterrupted and uncontested leadership allowed for organizational and financial stability, but it also inhibited questions and lively debate. In contrast with Butler's thirty-seven years as board chair, the four successive chairpersons presided for a total of eleven years. All of them were successful business people. Richard Rintelmann and James Wojmack were concerned about the financial health of Recovery Services and of Publishing. Louis Hill and Carol Pine envisioned Hazelden's future to lie in new initiatives and expansion into fields beyond chemical dependency.

Rintelmann and Wojmack emphasized and implemented a number of strategies they thought necessary not only for Hazelden's survival but also for its growth: succession planning, marketing, public policy, public relations, total quality management, contingency as well as strategic planning, the establishment of an endowment, ac-commodation to the boards of Hanley-Hazelden and New York, the selection of board members with particular expertise and talents, and, when necessary, staff reduction to balance the budget. Pater-nalism was a thing of the past. While respecting and acknowledging Pat Butler's genius and leadership, the new chairpersons as well as other board members wanted a stronger role for the entire board. They also presided over the changing of the guard from Swift to Spicer, which generated some turnover among senior management and board members.

When the board decided that Hazelden needed to assume a major role in the arena of public policy, Swift agreed in the fall of 1991 to resign as president and to assume the position of vice chair of Public Policy, a position he had held for two years, reporting directly to the chair of the board. When Swift announced his decision in a short speech to the crowded auditorium gathered in Bigelow, there was stunned silence. The change was unnerving and unexpected. Fol-lowing the silence, a spontaneous and thunderous round of applause erupted for an individual who was soon to celebrate twenty-five years of selfless service to Hazelden. The applause was well deserved. Swift came to Hazelden in 1966 at the invitation of Dan Anderson, five years after Anderson had become president, and he was stepping down from the presidency five years after Anderson had resigned. During those difficult years as administrator and pres-ident, Swift kept a steady hand on the rudder as he steered Hazelden through some very rough seas.

OPPOSITE:
Chairpeople of Hazelden's board

Patrick Butler, who served as president and chairperson 1952–1989 (top left)
Richard Rintelmann, 1989–1991 (top right)
James S. Womack, 1991–1994 (middle left)
Louis F. Hill, 1994–1997 (middle right)
Carol Pine, 1997–present (bottom)

Outside view of Tiebout Hall and meditation center on the Center City grounds. In the far background is the Bigelow Auditorium.
As Hazelden celebrates its fiftieth anniversary in 1999 and the new millennium rapidly approaches, the organization can look toward the future with many great strengths, especially its wealth of knowledge in the treatment of chemical dependency. The past has held immense challenges, and the future will surely present more.

4

Vision 2000

HAZELDEN'S HISTORY is marked by crises, some small, some large. Crisis is defined as a turning point when a state of things must soon terminate or suffer a material change. It is a decisive and crucial time, and some would describe it as a sacred time, an encounter with mortality. Finally, it is an ambiguous time, for one does not know what the final outcome will be. Crises can happen to both human beings and institutions. In this chapter the focus will be on Hazelden as an institution.

Crises may initially evoke confusion and a certain disorientation. This state can emerge either abruptly or as a subtle encroachment upon the person's or corporation's consciousness. One's normal way of acting has broken down, and the confusion that arises hints that something has to be reorganized. All sorts of warning signals alert the individual or the institution to the fact that it needs to adopt a new way of living or a new system for survival. It is a painful process that threatens the security to which one had become accustomed. As one looks back upon the crisis from the safe position that change and growth has created, one can see that from the initial chaos a positive and new way of thinking, feeling, and perceiving began to emerge.

This description of crisis, equally applicable to individuals and institutions, is a fairly accurate portrayal of the events that occurred at Hazelden from 1990 to 1994. The institution suffered confusion about what was occurring not only at Hazelden but also in the whole field of chemical dependency. Warning signals sounded the alarm that Hazelden had to replace an old way of providing services and doing business with a new system—a new way of thinking about its services and its customers. It could no longer take things for granted.

The signals came with increasing frequency. Educational Materials was unable to meet its revenue goals. The census of Rehabilitation Services continued to decline. Managed care was taking its toll. Profit margins disappeared and Hazelden had to nibble or dip into its reserves. Almost imperceptibly the building and grounds began to lose some of the luster and iridescence for which Hazelden was renowned. Staff downsizing, which was never considered, then thought of as a one-time event, was repeated thrice with a numbing regularity and a demoralizing effect. The closing of the Clinical Pastoral Education Program surprised staff and alumni alike and strained relations with some of Hazelden's most fervent supporters. Hazelden's future was in crisis. The warnings signaled the need for radical transformation, but no one was sure what that ought to be. And the pain touched everyone.

The Search for a President

In the autumn of 1991 the board launched a search for a new president, a search they hoped would be completed by the beginning of the new year. The fingerprints of the business people on the board were evident in both the process and the selection criteria. This would be the first time in the history of Hazelden that a board search committee and an outside consulting firm were involved in a presidential selection. Both Dan Anderson and Harry Swift had been the personal choices of Pat Butler.

The board had drawn up some very precise criteria for the consulting firm. Total quality management was to be the new hallmark of the Hazelden operation, even though this philosophy and practice was just beginning to be tested in health care organizations and had not yet been employed in the fields of mental health and chemical dependency. Public relations, marketing, and public policy were to be priority items for the new president. He or she would be expected

to restructure the organization for efficiency and effective communication. The board also expected the new president to turn Educational Materials and Hanley-Hazelden into healthy businesses. The board wanted the new president to work with and not against managed care whenever possible. The candidate needed to show a proven track record in total quality management and a proven ability to manage people. Above all candidates needed to demonstrate that they were results-oriented. The bias of the search committee was clearly in favor of an outside candidate, although internal candidates were not discouraged from applying.

In the meantime, to help manage the affairs of Hazelden during this troubling period of transition and to fill the vacuum of leadership, three senior management members were chosen to form the president's office. They were put in an awkward and almost paralytic position. It would have been inadvisable to make or even suggest any major decisions since the new president would be on board shortly, and the board itself began micromanaging many of Hazelden's operations. Frustration increased as the search for the new president dragged on.

Not everyone on the board was happy with some of the maneuvering that occurred during the search. Disappointed with the lack of progress in finding suitable candidates, the board fired the firm hired to conduct the selection process. The fact of the matter was that Hazelden was a formidable undertaking, and people experienced in the field as well as those outside the field were reluctant to commit themselves to the job, given the perilous environment and the downward spiral in which the chemical dependency field found itself. The eventual choice of an internal candidate was fortuitous because it guaranteed that no time would be lost in bringing the candidate up to speed on the intricacies of a complex organization. Presiding over Hazelden at a time of rapid change and uncertainty would be a monumental challenge.

Spicer's Leadership

Finally, in July 1992 Jerry Spicer was elected president and chief executive officer of Hazelden. Spicer possessed a thorough knowledge

Jerry Spicer,
president and CEO,
1992 to present

of Hazelden and its administrative bureaucracy, having served in a number of capacities since joining the organization in 1978. His experience at Hazelden included working in the areas of Research and Evaluation, Educational and Professional Services, and Employee Assistance. In 1988 he became senior vice president and chief operating officer under Harold Swift.

As the new president, Spicer brought to his task a well-developed business acumen, a tenacity for getting things done, and an in-depth knowledge of the national health care field. A logical thinker and clear communicator, he was a strong advocate of quality assurance and applied research (he has published extensively on these and other subjects). His plan and vision for the future of Hazelden corresponded very well with the board's exacting expectations of the new president. He was both pragmatic and determined, prepared to act upon whatever needed to be done to ensure the foundation's success. He was selected at a time when Hazelden needed strong and decisive leadership.

As he took office, Spicer was very conscious of the external forces that confronted Hazelden: increased competition, a weak economy, health care cost containment, negative public policy, rising costs, and employee uncertainty. He knew that to do nothing about these issues would guarantee more problems—even disaster and the ultimate demise of Hazelden. While he did not believe in change for

change's sake, he knew that adaptation and accommodation were necessary for Hazelden's survival.

Despite the numerous criteria that the board looked for in the new president, they all came down to one—the ability to restore the financial viability and health of the organization. Spicer, recognizing that Hazelden's success depended upon the foundation's principal revenue-producing centers, organized them into three major divisions: (1) Rehabilitation, (2) Educational Materials and Professional Services, and (3) Development and National Marketing. In addition, he created the Hazelden Institute under the direction of a vice chair. The institute had two principal branches: (A) Public Policy, whose mission was to influence the evolving health care policies on both the state and national levels in favor of coverage for chemical dependency treatment, and (B) Research, whose mission was to improve the treatment process by evaluating and demonstrating its effectiveness and to develop clinical pathways for the various patient typologies at Hazelden.

Spicer drew together a team that was able to respond to the major criteria that the board had formulated in the search for the new president. The executive vice presidents of the revenue-producing divisions, the vice chair of the Hazelden Institute together with the vice presidents of Human Resources and Finance formed the president's team. They were responsible for strategic planning and eventually became responsible for total quality management. Corporate leadership was replacing the leadership that had previously been provided by individuals who were charismatic and paternalistic.

Most of Spicer's team was composed of new players on Hazelden's stage. To survive, they faced a lot of obstacles. They needed to get a grip on the changes that had occurred and on how these changes could affect Hazelden's mission and philosophy as well as the direction of their own divisions. Without a history of parochialism inhibiting their efforts toward a common cause, the new vice presidents were finally able to overcome the negative perceptions that had persisted after the Byrd Report. Gradually, teamwork allowed them to make hard decisions and to do some much needed strategic planning based upon their collective vision and the board's expectations.

Beyond Crisis

Toward the end of 1993 Hazelden's situation began to ameliorate. Hanley-Hazelden revived to such an extent that by 1994 it was solidly successful. The most remarkable indicator of its success was when the center began to refer its excess admissions to Minnesota. Spicer's continued support of the senior management despite the financial disappointments of recent years allowed the facility and those in charge the time to find their niche in the community. It was refreshing to witness the Florida operation become a true community venture and not simply a Minnesota-managed operation. It was equally satisfying to see how the New York Fellowship Club benefited from the lessons learned at Hanley-Hazelden. The recruitment of its director and many of the staff from the New York metropolitan community helped the halfway house get off to a healthy beginning. By 1993 it had a full house and was on its way to financial viability, though it ran into trouble with managed care in subsequent years.

The success in New York further eased Hazelden's trepidation about expanding out of state. A partnership was formed with some of Hazelden's stakeholders in Chicago. Building upon the lessons that it had learned in Florida and New York, Hazelden initiated the venture and then provided the start-up capital, something that Hazelden previously had been reluctant to consider in its new ventures. Hazelden Chicago opened in January 1997 offering a complete range of outpatient and residential treatment options, family services, and continuing care, with a plan to expand into adolescent services, implemented in 1998.

In 1993, Rehabilitation Services began to recover from its admission doldrums. The division was reorganized and the name was changed to Recovery Services to signal Hazelden's desire to assist the chemically dependent and their families at any stage of their life-long recovery process, not just in rehabilitation. Special efforts were made to respond more expeditiously to client needs, including those within managed care systems. Some referents had developed a love-hate relationship with Hazelden. On the one hand they loved the outstanding care received by the patients they referred. On the other

hand, they sometimes encountered frustrating barriers in getting someone admitted. As a result, the admissions process was changed to facilitate a more rapid, respectful, and courteous entrance into treatment. To further accommodate referents and managed care groups, treatment on one of the units (Cronin) was partially redesigned to accommodate shorter lengths of stay.

A redesigned admissions process, a new case management system, renewed emphasis on public policy, public relations, and marketing, as well as the closing of other treatment centers outside of Hazelden—all contributed to a reversal of the decline in admissions. Beginning in 1994 the Recovery Services Division had several years of outstanding admission rates and gross revenues. The division was remarkably successful in representing its programs and locations as centers of excellence. That same year Hanley-Hazelden had its best year. The continuing success of the senior citizen program prompted the need for more beds. In response, the building that housed the skilled medical unit was expanded in 1998.

In 1997, continuing its tradition of providing separate units and specialized services for women, Hazelden opened up the Women and Children Recovery Community in New Brighton, a northern suburb of the Twin Cities. It serves as a safe and supportive residence for newly recovering chemically dependent women, particularly single women with children. Center City's Extended Care Program continues its national reputation for excellence and rarely has an empty bed. After the tough financial times in the late eighties and early nineties, patient aid actually increased, more than doubling in three years to $2.5 million in 1995. Thus, despite some difficult years, the Recovery Services Division still prides itself on its knowledge, experience, and research in providing, in the Butler tradition, the best care for the most people at the least cost.

Along with Recovery Services, other divisions also emerged from those transitional years of crisis to demonstrate resiliency. Public relations and public policy initiatives together with a substantial increase in marketing activities on the national level all contributed to making Hazelden a household name. The Responsibility of Friendship Program positioned Hazelden as the dominant player in turning around a major social and economic problem. If someone wanted to know anything at all about chemical dependency, all they had to do was phone "Ask Hazelden," where the Information Center answered every sort of question twenty-four hours a day, every day. This was followed in 1996 by Hazelden's appearance on the Internet, enabling browsers as well as Hazelden's stakeholders to gather up-to-date information on a variety of Hazelden-related topics.

Hazelden's public policy activities in Washington, D.C., and in Minnesota began to bear results. Before the total collapse of the national health care initiatives in 1994, all the bills issuing from congressional committees contained benefits for chemical dependency in one form or another. The 1998 Ramstad-Wellstone bill, the Substance Abuse Parity Act, seeks to pick up where previous initiatives ended.

In 1994 Development raised $4.5 million, and the Publishing Division managed to meet its revenue goals. By 1995 the fiscal crisis had passed. As one looks back on the events, the confusion and the disorientation were real as the organization groped to find a new system, a new way of dealing with the rapidly changing health care system, and new and innovative ways to serve those who sought Hazelden's help. Hazelden was reorganized around a talented team whose working together became the categorical imperative. Total quality management was introduced. Hazelden had become a recognized spokesperson on issues of national and state policy. Applied research was playing a substantial role in the formulation of clinical pathways and in the development of corporate goals. Marketing and development were having a significant impact on gross revenues. The Hazelden Pittman Archives gradually assumed recognition as a rich source for the history of alcoholism. Again, looking back upon the crisis, one can clearly see that a positive and new way of thinking, feeling, and seeing things had slowly emerged.

 Reflections on . . .
"To Be Happy, at Peace, and Glad to Be Alive"

I have a hard time explaining what's happened to me now that I'm sober. To have been brought out of how life used to be into the light of the way life is now is difficult to de-

scribe. It's as though I had spent my life inside a cage and never knew it. I couldn't realize what freedom was until I was released.

In my case, the timing for going to Hazelden was absolutely right. My life had utterly and completely fallen apart when I arrived there. The program started me back home. It's not that someone restored me to my old life, because my life today is completely new. And thank goodness for that because I don't want my old life back! I used to equate happiness with a lack of major problems in my life. Now I know what it means to be happy, at peace, and glad to be alive.

The changes are showing up in all parts of my life. My business was on the verge of bankruptcy, but now we're thriving and expanding. My wife was divorcing me and taking the children away from me, but now we're expecting our third child—my first child born in sobriety.

More important than business or family or any of the material things, however, is that I'm not carrying around that burden day after day of being ashamed of myself, of feeling like I'm a waste and a failure. Today, I live with myself, and I'm getting to like myself. That's the biggest change of all. And from this, all the other positive changes flow. People can tell you this, but in the end it has to come out of you—and it happened for me too—finally.

JOHN K.

Renewal of Trust among Staff

One final dimension of the crisis, however, still had to be resolved: the role and the changing nature of the caring community. More narrowly defined, it was the issue of staff morale and their belief during these years of crisis that their trust had been betrayed.

For years every attempt had been made to keep the board abreast on the affairs of Hazelden. In fact, this was one of Harry Swift's greatest strengths. Many of the board members prided themselves on what they considered their intimate knowledge of staff needs and their questions. Divisional committees would meet with assigned board members, who in turn would report back to the whole board. To keep their fingers on the pulse of Hazelden, they mandated a series of periodic audits during the eighties and nineties, the most famous of which was the Byrd Report.

Nonetheless, over the years a pattern of actions upsetting to the staff were approved by the board and implemented by senior management. Bonuses for sales staff and incentives for senior management were set in place. Gradually, this business flavor soured the attitude of many of the staff, who resented the fiscal favoritism shown to some, especially as their own compensation lagged and some benefits were curtailed. They felt that the response to the climate surveys and management audits never adequately addressed the issues of salaries and benefits. The annual board resolution thanking staff for work well done became a meaningless gesture in the background of cuts in the contributions to their pension plans and the increased employee share of costs for health insurance.

Staff layoffs in 1991 became the most telling blow to employee morale. This so-called voluntary exit plan reduced the workforce by some sixty employees. Middle management suffered a similar fate two years later. In 1995 Publishing was singled out for another downsizing. Paradoxically, what staff noticed during these years was that job postings remained abundant.

Board members seemed to be insensitive to, or unaware of, the confusion and disorientation of staff as the organization was passing from the culture of paternalism, through a new paradigm called total quality management, ending eventually in the pragmatic philosophy of partnership. Benevolent paternalism was an attitude on the part of the board and senior management based on the presupposition "We know what is best for you, and consequently we will take care of you." For a time it was successful in a family-like, small business operation. Over the years this culture of paternalism instilled in staff a sense of security. It was in the context of this spirit that Swift balked at the board's demand for staff reductions.

In defense of the board and its new business orientation, the thinking was that any morale problem would be erased by the paradigm of total quality management. But with its introduction in 1992, in the middle of crisis, it had the opposite effect. Instead of driving out fear, total quality management increased it. The idea of empowerment and the importance of employees in process improvement clashed with the downsizing that was occurring simultaneously. Staff had legitimate concerns about the amount of work that total quality management and the improvement process required over and above the expectations of their job descriptions and the extra work placed upon them by the loss of their associates. Signs increasingly pointed to the reality that staff was stressed out.

The amount of work seemed to be overwhelming: management audits and surveys, more surveys from the Joint Commission on the Accreditation of Hospitals, the expectations of successive board chairs imprinting their individual signatures on the organization, endless training seminars, new human resources and quality assurance plans, strategic planning—the mere recitation of the list begets a sense of exhaustion. Total quality management may have had the potential of relieving that stress with its emphasis on employee empowerment. However, getting to the point where staff are fully invested and responsible for the improvement of their own processes requires time, energy, and motivation that the individual employees simply did not have. They were particularly chagrined because they felt that no one was listening to them, despite the 1984 mission statement, which notes that Hazelden employees are essential to achieving the mission.

The nurses' call for a union in 1995 came as a real surprise to the board, whose immediate reaction was motivated in part by the strong dislike that some of the members had for unions rather than based on the issues upsetting staff. In the last analysis, the nurses felt that they were not being heard, a feeling resonated with the rest of staff as well. Haunted by the specter of a union on the Hazelden campus and its potential infiltration into other departments, the board requested that the president and his staff draft a corporate/employee relations plan to address the issues of communication with staff, of effective supervision, and of compensation.

The philosophy embodied in the 1996 Partners for Success declaration replaced the paternalistic culture and the caretaking philosophy of the previous decades. It attempted to resurrect the caring community core value through an emphasis on the partnership between employer and employee. It placed Hazelden squarely in the contemporary and changing environment where good business practices are necessary to sustain the growth and viability of any organization. Just as Hazelden had to have marketable products and services as well as skills at developing and delivering them, so do employees have the responsibility to continuously improve and develop new skills. This partnership with employees was based on the new rules of the work world with its infusion of total quality management. Employee empowerment became the new order of the day. Moreover, Hazelden committed itself to help employees enhance old skills and develop new ones. In this context then, the principles and practices of total quality management were but a means to an end and not an overarching culture.

Finally, to demonstrate that it meant business, the board approved the human resource plan whereby employees would receive an annual bonus if corporate goals, including a preset profit margin, were met through the efforts of the employees. In true business fashion, the board had finally instituted performance incentives to replace the annual paternalistic declaration of satisfaction with the good efforts of the staff.

In a certain sense, moving from paternalism to partnership as the new model for a caring community marked the end of the crisis. It also marked the beginning of a new stage of Hazelden's history that would witness in 1998 the reformulation of the 1985 mission statement, which now reads, "Hazelden will help build recovery in the lives of individuals, families, and communities affected by alcoholism, drug dependency, and related diseases."

As Hazelden, fortified with this new vision, moves toward the celebration of fifty distinguished and rewarding years, fifty years of passionate service for the chemically dependent and their families, one wonders: What will the future be like if Hazelden helps create it? What will it be like if left to others to forge? As it approaches the millennium, Hazelden is moving in two diverse but not necessarily incompatible directions: (1) the expansion of both treatment services and bibliotherapy for the recovery community, and (2) the expansion of services to those outside the recovery community (a renaissance of health promotion).

Reflections on . . .
"I Appreciate Everything a Lot More."

I used to go out all the time to dinner with girlfriends, and we'd drink all evening. We all drank too much, but I didn't really think much about what we were doing because we were all doing it together. I didn't really think I had any problem with drinking.

Finally, though, after a night on the town with some friends, I had a blackout and lost a favorite purse. I know this may sound trivial, that a lot of people have lost a lot more than a purse, but for me it was the signal I needed that maybe something was wrong and that I needed to take some action. I called my therapist, who suggested that I go to Hazelden Chicago for an evaluation.

I have to admit that when I went, I still didn't really think anything was wrong, and I half-hoped that they would agree so that I could keep doing what I was doing. I was very nervous about going. I didn't know anything at all about Hazelden. I didn't know anything, actually, about alcoholism or treatment, period. I was nervous, too, as I arrived. I wondered what would happen there. How would I be treated? Would I be badgered? Shamed?

Now I know that there was no need to worry. I was so impressed with the staff and the atmosphere of the place. I was treated with such respect and as an individual. I received a wonderful, but subtle, education there. No one was beating me over the head with anything. I just got the help I needed to see where my life was at and what I needed to do to change to make it better. To get well.

Hazelden and treatment are the best thing that's ever

happened to me. It probably saved my marriage. It certainly saved my life.

Friends say to me now, "Mary Ann, you seem happy." That's been a little surprising, because I had never had anyone tell me I was unhappy. I never thought of myself as an unhappy person. I actually thought my life was great. But others, of course, could see the pain and unhappiness, even though I couldn't.

Today, I appreciate everything a lot more. I take time to notice the little things—the spring flowers on a walk I take regularly, for example. I'm more contented and calm. Things that used to bother me don't anymore. Hazelden gave me a new lease on life, and I know that I'm really lucky.

MARY ANN M.

Recovery Services

Traditional treatment services—Hazelden's area of core knowledge and expertise—continue to confront challenges from both inside and outside the field. Health care will undergo a continuing consolidation of payers, providers, and insurers into large, well-capitalized for-profit systems that will be established on regional bases. Some form of managed care (results oriented, quality conscious, and cost effective) is here to stay, and health care in general will shift more and more away from residential care. But because the public can lose patience with quick fixes that are ineffective, those providers who can demonstrate the long-term effectiveness of their residential care will probably find a small stable market. The concept and implementation of centers of excellence should benefit Hazelden even though the multidisciplinary model will continue to be scrutinized and challenged as a nontypical provider of services. By demonstrating a regard for the whole person, Hazelden can offer a unique, high-quality treatment package in which chemically dependent people with multiple problems receive appropriate care before they are discharged.

The last five years have seen the treatment delivery system held more accountable to greater external control. The system is required to provide more for the patient with fewer resources. The era of care rationing does not exclude Hazelden. Pressure will be placed upon treatment systems to provide one-stop shopping, where the full range of inpatient, outpatient, education, and prevention services can be centrally located. This continues to be difficult for Hazelden, as the majority of its patients and families come from out of state. All the more reason for the expansion into regional centers.

As Hazelden approaches its fiftieth anniversary, clinicians should continue to integrate the growing body of data emerging from research with their own intuitive clinical understanding. Of particular importance will be the findings that evolve from its clinical pathways research suggesting appropriate lengths of stay for individuals who come to Hazelden. As part of the ever-growing professionalism of the field, clinicians will have to accept perform-ance standards based on individual patient need that are applicable to all service providers. The clinician training department will be challenged as it takes on more and more international trainees who have not been grounded in the self-help model. Particularly important to Hazelden's survival is a case management system that recognizes the ongoing nature of recovery: That primary treat-ment is but the beginning and not necessarily the most important stage of recovery. For long-term effectiveness, a good case manage-ment system presupposes constant follow-up or good referrals to community-based programs. Hazelden must continue to take bold and creative steps to serve the recovery community in all the stages of its journey.

Bibliotherapy plays an important role in ongoing recovery, and historically the Educational Materials Division has provided a core service. The future for Hazelden's publishing arm, however, will be bumpy. The question of whether Educational Materials should be an independent for-profit corporation or a respected and equal partner to Recovery Services recurs over and over again, and continually defies resolution. A separation would allow Educational Materials greater flexibility and less dependence on Recovery Services for its mission and direction. But renewed cooperation between Recovery Services and Publishing also holds some small potential. Examples of this were the cross-divisional cooperation in the publication of *The Way Home: A Collective Memoir of the Hazelden Experience* in 1997 and the use of Hazelden publications to strengthen the ongoing recovery of Hazelden patients.

Holistic Health—Body, Mind, Spirit

As Hazelden approaches its fiftieth anniversary, it faces the prospect of change as it moves in the direction of expanding Hazelden's services within and beyond the chemical dependency community. Pat Butler had anticipated this expansion in the eighties, urging the board to include other addictions, chronic illnesses, and related community services in Hazelden's mission. At that time, Dan Anderson predicted that Hazelden's future goal was to help improve the lifestyle of anyone who came in contact with Hazelden—not only to alleviate chronic diseases, including chemical dependency, but also to teach people of all ages to change their lives in positive ways. He was an ardent supporter of multiple approaches to health promotion. The board's expansion of the mission statement in 1998 fulfilled these prophecies. The expanded statement serves as a reminder of the importance of the holistic approach and of the need to make better use of Hazelden's multidisciplinary team. The fears of those who are uneasy about the broadened mission should be allayed by Hazelden's explicit statement of its continued commitment to the Twelve Step philosophy.

The Future of Publishing

Hazelden Information and Educational Services (the new title of Publishing, 1998) will seek to cast a wider net by helping professional and nonprofessional communities help others by providing necessary information to change people's lives. Its mission will be the promotion of holistic health that embraces body, mind, and spirit. As the

72

division looks toward the year 2000 and beyond, the tools to be used to fulfill its mission will be, besides printed information and training, use of Internet communications, electronic commerce, customized literature, print-on-demand technologies, as well as virtual reading rooms and chat room fellowship on the computer.

The Future of the Hazelden Model

As in the past, the board will continue to be confronted with a fundamental problem. It is both Hazelden's fiscal strength and its potential Achilles' heel—Hazelden's linkage to beds. What is meant by that statement? Today, in the health care field, the obvious and definite trend is away from bed utilization, whether chemical dependency, psychiatric, or acute care hospital beds. Is Hazelden's dependence upon bed utilization viable when the use of residential services continues to decline throughout the nation? Should the beds be used only for chemically dependent patients, or could some of them be diverted for other chronic illnesses or addictions? It is quite clear that managed care rarely pays for these inpatient programs. Would it be prudent to allocate some of the units to mental health clients when these residential programs are also in jeopardy? A decision to divert beds and diversify services could muddle Hazelden's reputation as centers of excellence for the treatment of chemical dependency.

Nonetheless, Hazelden's history clearly demonstrates that it has the heart and the courage to dare new things and move in directions where others feared to tread. Residential treatment is Hazelden's bread and butter. If Hazelden can demonstrate that other serious chronic illnesses need the environment that Hazelden provides for sustained and quality recovery, then its courage will be rewarded.

Does the Hazelden model have a future? The question has to be addressed in two parts: the future of the Hazelden model, and that of the residential program of twenty-eight days as one of the components of the Hazelden model. Given the multiplicity of forms that the Hazelden model has engendered, there is no reason to believe that it cannot continue to increase and multiply, shedding the outdated for the up and coming. But there is a caveat and a threat.

First the caveat. The Hazelden model will cease to exist if and when chemical dependency is no longer considered a primary illness but an appendage of mental health. Outside of the Hazelden family, the temptation is strong to do just that. Essential to the Hazelden model is the belief that addiction is not a mental health problem, but a distinct, primary chronic illness in its own right.

The threat comes from the public's attitude and perception. Efforts to respond to the national problem of chemical dependency over the past fifty years reinforces the axiom that history repeats itself. The treatment field faces a renewed moral dilemma with the recriminalization and restigmatization of the chemically dependent. The possible return of some societal specters loom ominously on the horizon: the societal attitude of labeling the alcoholic a loser, a reluctance to provide care on a continuing basis after an initial effort, a zero tolerance for illegal drugs, and decreased financial coverage for treatment. The present holds an eerie déjà vu quality. In the old days, presented in *Hazelden—A Spiritual Odyssey,* Austin Ripley, Lynn Carroll, Pat Butler, Dan Anderson, Harry Swift, and Gordon Grimm—following in the footsteps of Marty Mann (the woman who first spoke so eloquently on behalf of alcoholics)—went about telling the world that alcoholism was an identifiable illness, that alcoholics needed help and were worth helping. Now all the old barriers have been resurrected: the renewed conflict over the disease concept, the return of the stigma, the prisons with their revolving doors, the cultural hostility and intolerance. All the advances and contributions made by the Hazelden model and affiliates could be lost unless we regain public confidence and understanding.

Finally, there is the question: Does the residential Hazelden model, no matter how many days are involved, have a future? The original value of the model was that it permitted those who were ill enough the opportunity to get away to a controlled environment, where education, participation in a fellowship, and therapeutic engagement could occur. The question of whether twenty-eight days are essential is a nonissue if the program has a strong and proven case management system, is supported by research on a variety of clinical pathways to individualize the treatment, makes good use of community resources to allow for seamless treatment, and has in place a meaningful evaluation system demonstrating indisputable outcomes. Particularly important to its survival is a case management system that reinforces the concept that recovery is ongoing, that primary treatment is only the beginning and not necessarily the most important stage of recovery. At the same time, if residential treatment is to be an option, then the multidisciplinary team must be able to respond to the patient's collateral needs. In this day and age, the treatment of the whole person in the residential setting is an imperative.

Does the Hazelden model have a future? Let me remind you of a phrase in *Twenty-Four Hours a Day*, quoted from a Sanskrit proverb, with which I suspect most of you are familiar: "Look to this day, for it is life . . . yesterday is but a dream, and tomorrow is only a vision."

As it approaches the celebration of its fiftieth anniversary, Hazelden can look to the future with a great many strengths: a positive and solid reputation in the field, experience and durability, and the capacity for constructive change. Its major asset, of course, is its wealth of knowledge in the treatment of chemical dependency, garnered from both experience and research. Hazelden has the opportunity to continue its pioneering leadership by developing new services for tomorrow's health care market, continuing its regional expansion, building upon the strength of its national centers of excellence, and increasing its productivity through the implementation of its Partners for Success programs and through the findings of its clinical pathways research. As Jerry Spicer has noted, Hazelden's future depends in great measure on the leadership role that it exercises, its commitment to a holistic approach that embraces body, mind, and spirit, as well as its dedication toward innovation and the continuous improvement of its services.

Hazelden has explored new geographical frontiers due to the efforts of many, especially those people who are pictured here.

Top: Jack and Mary Jane Hanley, cofounders of the Hanley-Hazelden facility in West Palm Beach, Florida, pose with Nancy Graham (at left), mayor of West Palm Beach.

Middle: Larry and Nancy Beck, chief sponsors of Hazelden Chicago, pose with Peter Palanca (at right), Executive Director of Hazelden Chicago.

Bottom: Bill and Peggy Hassett, sponsors of Hazelden New York, at the 1997 Celebration of Hope.

5

Innocents Abroad

BY 1980 Hazelden was poised and ready for further growth and expansion. It had the resources at hand: money, stability, experience, knowledge, research, and the respect—even the envy—of the treatment community. More important, it wanted to help as many people as possible suffering from the illness of chemical dependency. People streamed to Hazelden as the mecca of the treatment world, coming for professional training and for consultation, advice, and information on the continuum of care for the chemically dependent. Many came simply to see the setting and experience the environment—to observe the originator of a very successful model.

The year 1981 marked the beginning of a new learning curve for Hazelden. Over the subsequent years, new centers offering a variety of services sprung up in the Twin Cities and then outside of Minnesota in Wisconsin, Florida, Texas, New York, and Illinois. In most instances the foundation experienced long-term successes, sprinkled with some short-term setbacks due to narrow judgment, poor personnel choices, and the inevitable clash of cultures. To some observers, Hazelden's seeming high-handedness evoked images of the "ugly American" in foreign lands. To others, the venture into additional locations, each with its own culture and customs, evoked the image of innocents abroad or of country folk in the big city. Through these challenges, Hazelden maintained a steadfastness of purpose and principle and found the courage to change and to learn from its mistakes.

Hazelden Center for Youth and Families

In the course of its history, Hazelden often felt challenged to help special populations too often neglected by the treatment field. Marty Mann played a role in influencing Pat Butler to open Dia Linn in 1956 in response to the needs of women. Young people were another group to which little attention had been paid. Although Hazelden had been treating some adolescents and young adults on its units at Center City since the late sixties, it was a difficult setting. Blending with the adult population was not a good mix. Adolescent acting out was often a major distraction. Conventional wisdom suggested that more than two adolescents on a unit could be a major disruption.

When Hazelden decided to take action on a larger scale by purchasing New Pioneer House in 1981, the venture became the foundation's first real test of merging with another complex culture. Situated in Plymouth, this rehabilitation center treated both adolescents and adults. It was the successor to the old Pioneer House, founded by Pat Cronin in 1948 to serve alcoholics in Hennepin County. As such it predated Hazelden by a year. A friend and disci-

Hazelden Center for Youth and Families in Plymouth, Minnesota

ple of Cronin's, Lynn Carroll found his own model for treatment in the simplicity of the Twelve Step program that Cronin had installed at Pioneer House.

When Hazelden purchased New Pioneer House the building was just three years old. Licensed for sixty-seven beds, the facility was located in a secluded wooded area shielded from the residential area of Plymouth. Architecturally its two treatment units were modeled upon the Hazelden units in Center City, even replicating the decorative fireplaces that adorn the comfortable lounge areas.

In 1990 Hazelden Pioneer House expanded its facilities and added a sixteen-bed skilled medical unit, an auditorium for lectures, and offices for staff. The skilled medical unit was the answer to a long-standing need. Until that time the center had no social space like Ignatia Hall in Center City, where the nurses could supervise those who were being detoxed or those who had extra medical problems.

In the early years of the merger, the two treatment centers were assessing each other. Although philosophically they were eminently compatible, as they were both based upon AA, they would encounter some differences. What New Pioneer House brought to the merger was experience and an enviable record in dealing with young

This statue of St. Francis formerly adorned a tree outside the Old Lodge and was relocated to Hazelden Center for Youth and Families.

people, who, as one board member reminded his associates, had special needs to which Hazelden needed to be extremely sensitive. The existing staff at New Pioneer House possessed that sensitivity to a remarkable degree. At the same time Center City, because of its long experience in the field, was able to enhance the treatment process to exceed the licensure and accreditation standards. To its credit and the ultimate satisfaction of all concerned, Hazelden decided very shortly into the venture that it would not continue to mix the adult and adolescent populations at New Pioneer House.

It was inevitable that the paternalism of Center City and the independence of New Pioneer House would clash. The latter was irritated with the encroachment of Center City upon its traditional way of doing things. It took pride in what it had already accomplished. Center City for its part took pride in its centralized administration with strong support services. But Center City's approach often seemed heavy handed, allowing its satellite operations little autonomy, initiative, and creativity.

Initially, some referents were reluctant to send young people to the new facility. These referents were comfortable with the program at Center City, and in some cases had undergone treatment there. If a referral was asked to leave—not a rare occurrence given the impulsiveness and the defiance of the population being treated—this reluctance was reinforced. There seemed to be less chance of dismissal at Center City. It took awhile to overcome this handicap, but by the mid-eighties New Pioneer House was beginning to gain national recognition for the treatment of young people, and referents began to acknowledge the wisdom of sending young people there.

At Hazelden, New Pioneer House patients were treated with dignity and respect—hard-line, confrontational tactics did not play a role in the treatment process. The corridors exuded a spirit of success and the expectation of the caring staff was that each patient could make it, that the Twelve Step program would work for young people as it did for adults. To this day, the graduation ceremonies continue to be moving for all the attendees—parents, friends, and clients. Emotional times are part of life at the center. Young people break the hearts of staff when they seem to be doing so well and it's discovered that they are using and are asked to leave.

Treatment is a serious matter, but it also has its lighter side. One patient came thousands of miles from the West Coast for help. Despite the admissions process and the luggage search, he managed to smuggle a special friend—his pet rabbit—into his semi-private room. When his roommates discovered E.T., they said the rabbit would have to go through admissions. When the proper authorities observed no loss of control indicators, they concluded that E.T. was not a candidate for treatment. E.T.'s owner was saddened beyond belief. When the matter was brought to the executive director, he perused all of the licensures to see if any exception could be made, but to no avail. E.T. had to go. Finally, common sense and compassion prevailed. A sensitive staff member took the enchanting rabbit home until his master could complete treatment.

A great strength that Pioneer House brought to the merger with Hazelden was the spirit of a caring community. Over the years Pioneer House was able to maintain this spirit and serve as a model for Center City, which risked losing the same quality as it increased in staff and expanded its locations.

In 1993 Pioneer House's name was changed to the Hazelden Center for Youth and Families, and the facility had positioned itself within the Hazelden continuum as a center of excellence. This growing recognition throughout the United States can be attributed to many factors, including the center's special assessment process, the peer process, the development of its own Parenting Program, and the addition of the Outpatient Counseling Clinic.

ASSESSMENT PROCESS

One of the most singular strengths of Hazelden's Center for Youth and Families is its assessment process. It is critical to know what exactly is going on with young people when they are admitted. Treatment demands a staff versed in the developmental stages of young people, a staff capable of assessing and prioritizing the many problems that young people bring with them, and a staff gifted with great patience and compassion.

Adolescence is a time of impulsive, oppositional, and unstable behavior. It is the time when personal fables develop. The egocentricity of adolescents supports their personal conviction of their own uniqueness, their own infallibility, and especially their own indestructibility. Watching an adolescent "hot dog" on a ski run, one realizes that the concept of powerlessness does not come easy for those who believe they can do anything and who are determined to investigate their own infinity. Young people are a particularly difficult population to treat. Daring, dangerous, and crazy behavior come easily to the adolescent. When this is compounded by the use of chemicals and the high that they provide, the Center for Youth and Families has a double dose of problems to deal with.

One of the major consequences of adolescents' substance abuse is the retardation of their social and emotional maturity. The adolescent developmental tasks of defining self and sexual identity, of building peer relationships, and of separating appropriately from families are difficult enough even when chemicals are not present. When young people begin to depend on chemicals, their growing-up process is obstructed and they do not develop the skills needed to cope in the adult world. Many never finish high school and do not know how to deal with their emotions in positive ways, how to complete tasks, or how to socialize without drugs.

Along with a history of chemical use and stunted developmental growth is the possibility of a serious mental or emotional disturbance. The priority for clinicians is to sort out the primary problem of anyone seeking admission. Is the young person acting out and using chemicals to get through the adolescent stages? Is the young person truly chemically dependent? Is there a concurrent mental health problem such as depression, anxiety, obsessive compulsiveness, or attention deficit disorder? A whole-person assessment is needed— not just a snapshot of a person taken and developed within an hour, but a running video that captures the young person in multiple stages and multiple dimensions.

In the mid-eighties a correct diagnosis was the order of the day. Despite its in-depth multidisciplinary assessment process, the Center for Youth and Families saw the need for an even better tool to sort out the symptoms and to do a proper diagnosis, thereby satisfying the critics of chemical dependency treatment. During 1986 and 1987 the center became a major participant in the research and development of a reliable and accurate assessment tool. Funded by the St. Paul Foundation, the Personal Experience Inventory was completed in 1988 and received national acclaim as a holistic tool. The inventory enabled counselors to discern whether a patient's chemical use was simply abuse or serious dependency, whether mental health was an issue, and whether both issues were present at the same time (dual diagnosis). Or they may have been simply acting out behavior associated with the developmental tasks characteristic of an adolescent or young adult population.

Hazelden's participation in the development of such a tool came at a propitious time. Adolescent treatment, both mental health and chemical dependency, was undergoing severe scrutiny by the national media and by government agencies in the late eighties. The charge laid against the treatment centers, sometimes proven sometimes not, was that they were improperly diagnosing and admitting young people into residential treatment and holding them there so that they could keep their beds full. The Center for Youth and Families came through the intense scrutiny with its reputation unscathed, principally because it could demonstrate that it did thorough assessments and well-founded diagnoses.

 Reflections on . . .
"Who'd Have Ever Guessed?"

I was a patient at the Hazelden Center for Youth and Families in 1994, and I still remember everyone so well. I was really sick and in pretty sad shape, suffering from heroin and alcohol addiction. My counselor was super and made such a big difference in my life. Actually, everyone there did.

So here I am, still sober after these four years, and loving life! I am back in college, pursuing my degree in English literature and having a ball. I attend AA meetings regularly, have a wonderful sponsor, and am actually sponsoring a few people myself. Who'd have ever guessed? I'm also engaged to be married soon.

I'm so grateful that I was able to get my start at

Hazelden. Going there saved my life. I really cannot possibly tell you how wonderful my life is now. . . . I just can't find the words to explain it.

STEPHANIE W.

PEER PROCESS

In keeping with adolescent and young adult needs, the Center for Youth and Families has been eminently successful in the use of a peer process. From its inception, the center has used the peer process to determine whether young people understood and accepted the reality of their own powerlessness over the use of chemicals. Patients had to present the First Step to peers as well as to the counselor to demonstrate that they knew what they were talking about and not just manipulating the process. The peers could then accept or reject this First Step and provide the reasons for the judgment. Once peers had accepted the First Step, patients could continue their treatment. It was a very effective dynamic.

Peer involvement and positive peer pressure play a very constructive role in the recovery and continuing care process. In listening to each other's stories and Step presentations, and in challenging each other's thoughts and actions, peers serve as healthy mirrors for each other. Patients begin to understand why they should be sober once they start talking to other young people who are further advanced in the treatment process and feeling confident about their own recovery. They begin to see the possibilities for an enjoyable and productive life that recovery offers them.

While managed care's belief that one-on-one counseling could be just as effective as the peer process in severe cases of chemical dependency was hardly demonstrable, the Center for Youth and Families did expand its continuum of care to accommodate some of the concerns of the managed care companies. Young people can now access a wide range of services that include residential and outpatient assessment and evaluation, residential and outpatient primary treatment, a less expensive extended care program, a parent program, continuing care, and an outpatient counseling clinic.

OUTPATIENT COUNSELING CLINIC

The number of young people arriving at the Center for Youth and Families with dual diagnoses continues to grow at an alarming rate. For this reason, the center petitioned the State of Minnesota in 1993 for a license to establish a mental health outpatient clinic. This new counseling clinic allowed the center to be more responsive to concurrent problems.

The clinic is also an important prevention and educational resource on chemical dependency for the community at large and especially for parents. The holistic approach and continuum of services at the Center for Youth and Families have been a model for Center City to imitate. Indeed, Center City established its own counseling clinic in 1995 to respond to the needs of clients in both primary and continuing care.

THE PARENTING PROGRAM

The strong centralization exercised by Center City was never more pronounced than in the way it exercised control over the Family Program at the Center for Youth and Families. For years Center City would not allow the development of a family program specific to the needs of young people and their parents. Parents were required to attend the Family Program at Center City, even though their sons and daughters were at the center fifty miles away. After nearly a decade of intense, sometimes acrimonious debate, Center City finally recognized that the needs of parents and their adolescent children were different from those of families of adult children. The Center for Youth and Families entitled its family services the Parenting Program. The education and the sharing involved therein have been very effective—the healing process that occurs is gratifying for all participants.

Like the healing process of its clients, the merger between the Center for Youth and Families and Center City went through its own healing process. Effective leadership demanded administrators loyal to Hazelden and knowledgeable about its history, goals, and philosophy but also flexible enough to appreciate the traditions of the culture being assimilated. Despite the inevitable bickering between the two sites, the merger was a resounding success. Excellent leadership at the center and the gradual loosening of the tight reins from Center City allowed the creativity of the Center for Youth and Families to emerge in services such as the Parenting Program.

Hanley-Hazelden

The successful merger that occurred with New Pioneer House encouraged the Hazelden Board of Trustees to entertain the possibility of expansion beyond Minnesota. A wealth of experience had been gained and senior management assured board members that Center City had the technology and the managerial resources to move into other areas. But the confidence was misplaced and the assurances were misleading, for the endeavor that was to follow in Florida was an entirely new and different experience. Hazelden seemed to be cursed by the belief that any new venture anointed with the Hazelden mission was bound to be successful. Center City's inability to clearly define the scope and purpose of the Hanley-Hazelden board in relationship to Hazelden and its board almost caused the demise of the new venture.

The driving force behind the expansion into Florida was Jack Hanley, the very successful and soon-to-be-retired president of Monsanto. Grateful for a recovery in his immediate family, and the resulting serenity and happiness that enveloped the family, he and his wife, Mary Jane, wanted to help others share a similar experience. He sensed that the West Palm Beach community to which he was retiring might be a good place to establish a treatment center. Others assured him that the need was there, and he and his wife agreed that Hazelden would be the ideal foundation to establish it.

In 1982 Hanley approached Dan Anderson, whom he described as the "wise old owl," about the possibility of collaborating with him in setting up a center in Florida replicating Hazelden's services. Anderson said that Hazelden would be willing to provide the technical assistance in a consultative fashion if the community there expressed the need and provided the financial backing. A feasibility study demonstrated the need, and Hanley assured Anderson that the money would be raised within the community. He hired a development person, shrewdly donated $1 million to the United Way, half to the national office and another half to the West Palm Beach County office. He calculated, quite correctly, that the community's donors would thereby be receptive to his requests for donations for his own venture.

However, a mere consultative role on the part of Hazelden was not to his liking. He wanted Hazelden both to install and to manage a whole continuum of traditional and innovative services. Realizing that it had a committed sponsor, the Hazelden board agreed in 1983 to be a full partner in the undertaking.

From that point forward things moved quickly. An outpatient program, the first part of a continuum of services, was installed in 1984. A $5 million fundraising campaign ran concurrently with the planning for a new sixty-bed residential treatment program. A modern and beautiful facility was constructed replicating the functionality of Center City but adapted to Florida's culture and climate. St. Mary's Hospital, prompted by a need to do something for the chemically dependent as well as by Hazelden's reputation, donated the land. The community's support was manifested with the successful conclusion of the development campaign. Everything was in place for the dedication of Hanley-Hazelden Center at St. Mary's, which

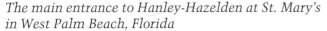

The main entrance to Hanley-Hazelden at St. Mary's in West Palm Beach, Florida

occurred in October 1986 before a large audience with former First Lady Betty Ford delivering the principal address.

It was inconceivable that the new venture would be anything but successful given the financial backing and Hazelden's reputation for longevity in the turbulent field. Euphoria carried the day, just as it carries patients who complete the Fifth Step in treatment. That euphoria quickly gives way to the reality of living a life of sobriety in the real world, with its struggles and temptations.

In part, Hanley-Hazelden suffered an image problem. Like the Center for Youth and Families, Hanley-Hazelden struggled against the perception that treatment in Florida was somehow inferior to that provided by Center City. Beyond this similarity, however, the experience gained at the Center for Youth and Families proved of little avail in managing a facility two thousand miles from Center City. From the Center for Youth and Families, Hazelden had inherited a tested program with an organizational structure, competent staff, and the whole range of support services; and, for its part, Hazelden provided the youth center with talented and dedicated administrators. In the case of Hanley-Hazelden nothing was in place, nothing was inherited. Hazelden was starting with a clean slate. One might think that given these circumstances the new venture would have smooth sailing. Unfortunately, the problems that ensued were much more formidable than those encountered with the merger at the Center for Youth and Families. Managed care, a complicated governance structure, and personnel problems would all sorely try Hanley-Hazelden in its first years.

MANAGED CARE

Early on Hanley ran into problems with managed care, which was already making inroads in Florida. As he was making his rounds of Florida chief executive officers for financial support and patient referrals, Hanley was repeatedly asked why he was bringing in and relying on the twenty-eight-day treatment model. Their employee assistance programs felt that inpatient/outpatient or simply outpatient programs were just as effective and even more cost effective. Hanley assured them that Hazelden would be flexible enough to accommodate the growing concerns of managed care and their needs for reduced lengths of stay. But Hazelden's initial unwillingness or inability to accommodate haunted and frustrated Hanley in the coming years.

GOVERNANCE STRUCTURE

The complicated governance structure at Hanley-Hazelden also proved problematic. What began as a separation and balance of powers eventually led to confusion and detracted from the expectations of dedicated leadership. The corporate board was composed of members from the three founding corporations: (1) St. Mary's Hospital, which contributed the land and elected six trustees to the board; (2) the Hanley-Hazelden Foundation, responsible for fundraising and development, elected three trustees; and (3) the Hazelden Foundation, responsible for managing and developing the program, elected three trustees. While the three partners had ultimate responsibility for Hanley-Hazelden, it was not clear how those responsibilities differed from those of the twelve trustees. No one paid much attention to the three-headed hydra until the center ran into troubled financial waters.

Despite a shaky beginning, Hanley-Hazelden is a success today in treating older adults, in part because of the camaraderie, fellowship, and sense of dignity and respect toward chemically dependent people carried over from Center City, Minnesota to West Palm Beach, Florida.

89

Jack Hanley correctly perceived in the early eighties that the West Palm Beach community would be an idyllic spot to establish a treatment facility. Many older adults and others have Hanley to thank for his vision.

Personnel

Hanley-Hazelden's first executive director, who had done an excellent job in cultivating the West Palm Beach community, became seriously ill and was forced to take a medical leave after three years. Other members of the management staff were too inexperienced and lacked the vision and the inspiration needed to lead the program. Although the Hazelden board had been led to believe that there were half a dozen competent staff members in Center City capable of running the new program, Hazelden was unable to recruit a program manager from within its staff, someone who had personal experience with the treatment program as it had evolved over the years and who could further that evolution at Hanley-Hazelden with new ideas and new services. This deficit in leadership led to rapid turnover of senior management, which weakened program stability and continuity. In addition, caution had not been used in hiring support staff. Everyone wanted to work at Camelot, and everyone wanted to counsel patients even though they were not hired to do so. The management difficulties at Hanley-Hazelden set the stage

90

for conflict between Florida and Center City, both at the management and the board levels.

CONTROL FROM CENTER CITY

The geographical separation kept Center City from getting a good handle on the situation and the needs of Hanley-Hazelden. The management turnover broke down communication links between the two centers. Hanley-Hazelden resented Hazelden's rigid imposition of policies and procedures without input from the Hanley-Hazelden staff. They felt that Center City not only wasn't providing them with enough resources but also did not know what was happening in West Palm Beach. Center City would fly in senior management, who would stay a short time and then fly home. To protest what they perceived to be a shortage of staff, Hanley-Hazelden staff would not fill all the beds on their units. This contributed to budget shortfalls, which became a regular yearly occurrence.

The situation came to a head in 1990, when the new executive director sought to impose Center City's will on the Hanley-Hazelden staff. Both internal and external grievances were filed, anonymous hate mail was found on the desks even of the neutrals, antagonists would not speak to one another without tape recorders. Feelings of suspicion, anxiety, frustration, and depression pervaded the corridors. It was not a serene environment. The strict adherence to doing things the Center City way contributed in large measure to the struggles that Hanley-Hazelden was undergoing.

It was a wonder that Hanley-Hazelden survived 1990, which saw the resignation of yet another executive director, a staff turnover of some thirty-five people (preceded by forty-five in 1989). What was particularly painful was that the quarrel and its divisiveness spilled into the community, testing the allegiance of even the most loyal Hazelden supporters. There is no doubt that the struggle diminished some of the community support for the program and that the Hazelden name was tarnished. Some were shocked by the rumors, innuendoes, and public accusations, and some were saddened by the truth that a good cause was in peril.

Like the addicted person, Hanley-Hazelden had to have its own death-rising experience. Despite the fractured staff and internal dissension, patients continued to come and the center continued to expand. The Kootz Education Center was built, providing a lecture hall, quarters to house the Family Program, a bookstore, and recreational facilities. Nonetheless, by the end of 1990 it became clear that Hanley-Hazelden was engaged in a serious struggle to survive the impacts of a negative external environment, of management discontinuity, of the alienation of referral sources, and of the erosion of local community support.

CUTTING THE UMBILICAL CORD

In 1991 Center City installed a new senior management team. Swift and Spicer were finally ready to cut the umbilical cord that threatened to strangle the new endeavor and entrust the new management team with the task of turning Hanley-Hazelden around. The Hanley-Hazelden management team finally had the freedom to be more flexible and innovative in meeting the needs of the center and its clients, but it took a fiscal crisis severe enough to almost cause the collapse of the venture. Since its inception Hanley-Hazelden's operating losses—including almost $1 million in 1991—had been covered by Hazelden. Because the board in West Palm Beach had not been providing input into the financial and long-range strategies of Hanley-Hazelden, Center City had assumed more and more responsibility. It was a catch-22 for all involved. By playing banker and assuming the center's losses, Hazelden reinforced the image that the board in West Palm Beach was merely a social gathering. In reality the trustees felt left out of the decisions that Hazelden appeared to be making on its own. And Hazelden felt guilty for what many believed was its mismanagement. Eventually the Hazelden board acknowledged its own responsibility for Hanley's lack of success and profitability and noted the two other partners (St. Mary's and Hanley-Hazelden) would have to demonstrate a willingness to play a more active role.

Subsequent meetings held at the end of 1992 to discuss the financial plight of the center involved the partners from St. Mary's Hospital, Hanley-Hazelden, and the Hazelden Foundation. The heated discussions revolved around Hazelden's management skills, the debt owed to Hazelden in excess of $1 million, and the fact that a fundraising campaign could be construed as an attempt to raise money from the West Palm Beach community to send back to Minnesota for a debt that many thought was clearly the result of poor management on Hazelden's part. From the anger, finger-pointing, disenchantment, and confusion, there eventually emerged a desire to clarify issues and work for the best interests of the center. The partners agreed that while Hazelden was the manager of the center, its financial viability and mission were the responsibility of all three partners.

The partners agreed to share responsibility for meeting cash flow needs up to an agreed upon amount. They endorsed a fundraising campaign and reduced Hazelden's management fee. The partners also decided that the next chair of the board would be a member of the West Palm Beach community. The new Hanley-Hazelden executive director appointed in 1992 was talented, experienced, and very well respected in the Florida community. Under his direction the staff stabilized and a whole range of new programs was created.

By 1994 Hanley-Hazelden was treating more patients than ever, and its profit margin was 17 percent. It was able to pay back a good portion of the debt it owed to Hazelden. The success could be attributed to strenuous marketing efforts, good planning, the introduction of total quality management, community involvement, and especially excellent leadership.

The campus now includes a medical unit for detoxification and assessment, a day treatment program, an evening outpatient program, adult residential programs, a residential and day program for senior citizens, a relapse program, an adult intermediate care facility (halfway house), and a family program. Community and professional education workshops and an array of aftercare services are also offered.

Hanley-Hazelden's reputation as a center of excellence is derived particularly from the fine treatment it provides for senior citizens. In a community with a large elderly population, the center responded to an increasing need for additional services with a modified, slower-paced treatment regimen for older adults. Special medical needs are attended to, rest periods are scheduled daily, there are fewer reading assignments and less paperwork, and group therapy sessions address issues of special importance to this population, such as grief and loss.

The task to turn Hanley-Hazelden around took three years, but the support of the three partners and of the new president of Hazelden, Jerry Spicer, remained steadfast. A major reason for the eventual success of Hanley-Hazelden was that the community was allowed to take ownership and become an important stakeholder in the venture. It became a community-based program. The lessons learned from the history of the Hanley-Hazelden undertaking would prove to be very valuable as Hazelden moved into new geographic areas such as New York and Chicago.

Fellowship Club-New York: A Home Away from Home

Given Hazelden's strong alumni base in the Northeast, this region had long held a special attraction for such expansion. In New York referrals totaled about 20 percent of all the Hazelden admissions for the year 1989. Thus, when a potential relationship with Tufts Medical School failed to develop, some of Hazelden's key New York alumni expressed a strong desire that Hazelden find another way to establish a presence in New York, where there was an obvious need for the treatment and quality of care for which Hazelden was known.

In May 1989 an advisory committee was formed composed of alumni and other prominent people who knew about Hazelden's work with chemical dependency. This important social issue affected New York mightily. The advisory committee was chaired by Bill Hassett, who, together with his wife, Peggy, was keenly aware of the ravages that chemical dependency could inflict upon society at large and families in particular. As a couple, they were two of Hazelden's staunchest advocates.

The first question that the committee tackled was what service would best respond to New York's many needs. They quickly concluded that it would not be wise to try to duplicate Hazelden's primary program in New York, because this would only siphon off referrals to Center City. Some time was spent considering whether

94

The front entrance to Hazelden New York, New York City

Clapton Hall—the lecture hall at Hazelden New York

to establish a center for adolescents, but that idea was set aside when the committee learned how much was already being done for young people. The concept of a halfway house finally took hold. The strong argument in favor of it was that the facility would serve the needs of patients coming out of primary treatment in the New York area as well as of patients returning from treatment in Minnesota. The decision to proceed with a halfway house was unanimous, and a task force was formed to find an appropriate site.

Initially a location outside Manhattan was favored, but the committee soon realized that there would be overwhelming opposition from middle-class neighborhoods, which wanted no part of alcoholics and drug addicts. The name Hazelden meant nothing to them. This prompted an earnest search for a location in Manhattan. After visiting about sixty potential sites, the task force was approached by the real estate agent with whom it had first consulted about a former convent on the lower East Side that now belonged to the Salvation Army. The agent had previously informed the task force that he already had a buyer for it. But now, sixty visits later, he said that it was once again available and at a reduced price. The reduced price took some of the sting out of the expenditure of so much wasted energy. Moreover, by visiting so many other potential sites, the deficiencies noted in these buildings served to confirm the strengths of the Salvation Army building, located at 220 East Seventeenth.

The most difficult question now was how to pay the building, renovation, furnishing, and start-up costs. Hazelden's expectation, just as with Florida, was that the community would raise the money before purchasing and opening the facility. The advisory committee had agreed to this initially. But in order to open as soon as possible New York believed that the financial backing should be a joint undertaking, with Hazelden providing initial bridge money that would be repaid as quickly as possible. The investment would be a sign of Hazelden's commitment to the project. By the middle of 1991 there was a good faith agreement on the part of Hazelden to do this, but as the year moved on some of the Hazelden board members grew reluctant to follow through. The office of the president was vacant, a new board chair had been recently elected, and Hanley-Hazelden was losing $1 million.

At the December board meeting a variety of suggestions were made: (1) that the New York start-up be pushed back; (2) that another less expensive site be sought; and (3) that, given the environment unfriendly to the chemical dependency field and the losses that Hazelden was suffering, the New York venture be abandoned.

The reaction in New York to these suggestions was not unexpected. Hazelden was in danger of alienating a very loyal and supportive segment of stakeholders who had worked hard and long toward making the Fellowship Club a reality. Hazelden agreed to advance the money, the property was purchased, and the facility opened in October 1992. A fundraising event held in May 1993 greatly alleviated the anxiety about finances. Foundations and chief executive officers took notice when it was announced that Liza Minelli would be the featured entertainer. How did little, unknown Hazelden manage that? Even New Yorkers were impressed. The event, the accompanying publicity (a full-page spread in *The New York Times* social section), and the substantial amount of money that had been raised ($1 million) augured well for Hazelden's expansion into the Northeast.

The first three patients in the fifty-five-bed facility were Hazelden referrals, two from Extended Care in Center City and one from Hanley-Hazelden. By the end of the year, all thirty-five beds opened in the first stage of planning were full. Past learning experiences served the new venture well: The executive director chosen to lead the program was hired from New York City applicants. She was a tested performer, very familiar with the New York chemical dependency network. Center City's contribution was a manager and a few clinicians who knew the Hazelden model and technology. It was a realistic and solid attempt to blend the two cultures—New York and Minnesota.

Growing pains are a given in any undertaking. The Hazelden-trained staff obviously knew how to run a halfway house, based on the Hazelden model of respecting the dignity of each individual patient. This was an essential core value of Hazelden treatment. But many of the newly hired staff from New York's multicultural community came from a therapeutic background accustomed to dealing with patients in a hard-nosed if not demeaning fashion. Their stance was that Hazelden did not know how to deal with New Yorkers.

Much can be made of the cultural differences between New York and Minnesota, but this can also be exaggerated. Minnesotans think that New Yorkers like to hear themselves talk, are cheeky with their bold statements, and are arrogant in their assumptions and conclusions. New Yorkers think Minnesotans are too guarded, noncommittal, and snail-like as they crawl to decisions. In short, Midwesterners think New Yorkers are arrogant; New Yorkers find the Midwestern "nice" tepid and turgid.

All things considered, whatever the variations in tonality and style, it did not take long for the staff at Fellowship Club to resolve their differences and build tolerance and respect for different styles and approaches as they slowly but surely created a caring community similar to that in Minnesota. New Yorkers respected the know-how of the Minnesotans; the latter respected the insights of the New Yorkers; both respected and benefited from the others' care and compassion for patients.

The whole staff experienced pressure from other areas. While the official word was that a full census was not the expectation for the first year, the unspoken word was full occupancy. The pressure became intense, given the number of patients with multiple diagnoses who entered Fellowship Club and the high number of patients who had not had sufficient primary care. Consequently, a high discharge rate at staff request was not unusual. This, of course, ran counter to the expectation of keeping the beds full.

Good clinical practice and a good profit margin were not always compatible. It could put the clinicians in an awkward position. If the patient was discharged, the counselor was held accountable rather than the patient. On the other hand, by allowing contrary patients who should have been discharged to remain in treatment, the clinicians could be accused of "enabling" the patients and contributing to the disruption of the caring community at Fellowship Club. The pressure increased when bonuses were paid to senior management for higher profit margins. To address the problem, New York developed a more intensive two-to-three-week track within the halfway house to respond to the needs of those patients who had not had adequate primary treatment. Because of its low cost, it had a definite appeal to some managed care companies and harbingered a future model of treatment—a supplemental primary program within a halfway house setting.

There were also pressures to accommodate managed care and employee assistance program counselors, who would dictate treatment plans and timetables for discharges. Gradually, however, the multidisciplinary teams at Fellowship Club took control of the treatment planning and the process.

Financial problems developed in the beginning, when too many patients were given free or discounted care, and inordinately large discounts were given to managed care companies. Some indigent people viewed Fellowship as a food pipeline for their whole families, and lunchtime guests sometimes surpassed the number of Fellowship patients. The staff resolved these issues by establishing clear financial and treatment requirements for admission. The intent was to work with managed care without being controlled by it.

Fellowship Club demonstrated resiliency and creativity on other fronts, as well. At the very time that Hazelden was suffering severe setbacks in its Employee Assistance, Health Promotion, and Outpatient Programs, Fellowship Club took the Center City model for the Physicians in Residence Program, revised it, and intensified its experiential component. Funding for the program came from the Josiah Macy Foundation, which provided a three-year grant, worth $460,000, to educate thirty-two interns (fourth- and fifth-year medical students) each year.

The first year of operation was such a great success that the program was unable to accommodate all the candidates that applied in the two subsequent years. The Macy Foundation was so impressed by the success of the program that it granted another $95,000 to develop an evaluation component to test the knowledge and ability of the doctors who went through the program against that of those who did not. The outcomes enhanced the program's credibility and have the potential of making some form of chemical dependency training a licensure requirement for primary care physicians. This, of course, would have an enormous impact on the treatment of chemical dependency, and Hazelden would have added another educational component to its continuum of services.

Physicians often confront alcoholics and drug addicts in emergency rooms, where they can easily conclude that these people are hopeless cases. The interns who participate in the residency program at Fellowship Club come into personal contact with recovering people. The week-long, highly intensive, program is comprised of lectures given by physicians and Fellowship Club staff on the nature of the illness, its diagnosis and treatment, and the components of the Minnesota Model. But it is the personal encounter with the patients—their groups, their stories of unmanageability, and their AA meetings—that convinces the doctors of the power of chemicals and the powerlessness of the patients addicted to them. By listening to the patients' stories, the interns discover that these are good human beings who have a treatable illness and who are capable of change. "As medical residents, we get a skewed picture of who's chemically dependent," said one of the residency participants who attended the program. "We see certain kinds and severities of chemically dependent people—mainly the socially disabled, chronic drug users who keep coming back. It's hard to imagine them ever getting healthy and functional. You see them come into emergency rooms drunk, repeatedly, so it's easy to adopt an attitude of 'why bother?' But this training program helps you see beyond that. You see chemically dependent people who have gotten their act together—people who are doing their own laundry, getting jobs, staying sober, and rejoining the human race."

Like Hanley-Hazelden, New York Fellowship Club underwent a refining process. A decline in referrals, pressures by managed care, rapid changes in senior management, and budget shortfalls led to some soul-searching about governance and control and the need for more autonomy for New York.

The programs that Fellowship Club developed and its innovative responses to growing pains led to a healthier, more focused, and stabilized community. The deep rewards associated with the work—seeing people change and get healthy—united the staff in a common purpose, providing patients with "a home on the way home." Gradually the Fellowship Club alumni grew in numbers and the Friday night gatherings, which resembled the popular model in St. Paul, became a central happening in the New York recovery community. From these gatherings a transition group evolved for those who needed extra help during the early stages of recovery after graduating from the club.

Hazelden Chicago

During strategic planning meetings in the eighties, Chicago's name always seemed to come up. In fact, the Chicago-Milwaukee axis was the prime choice when Hazelden considered expanding in 1964, but instead the board decided to construct new units at Center City. Chicago was Hazelden's strongest referral, sending literally thousands of patients over the years to Center City. Hazelden's expansion into New York would not be left unchallenged by the five thousand alumni in the Windy City.

Hazelden's commitment to Chicago started in January 1993, when it opened an office at 212 West Superior Street. That site served as a resource center for Hazelden alumni and others in recovery. Continuing care groups, educational workshops, alumni events, and AA meetings were held there. Screening and referral services were also offered.

In 1994 staff at the facility conducted a needs assessment of chemical dependency services in the Chicago area, which confirmed that the demand for addiction services was not being met. In January 1995 the Hazelden Board of Trustees approved plans for the Chicago expansion. In October of the same year more than $500,000 was raised to finance the new project. Again learning from past experience, Hazelden agreed to supply the bridge money to begin the project. Expected to cost $6 million, the plan included the purchase of the building, renovation and start-up costs, and funding for a patient scholarship fund.

The site, which encompasses three buildings (the former Russian Embassy and two smaller adjoining buildings) is located at the north edge of the Chicago Loop at 867 North Dearborn. An ideal location, the site allows people from Chicago and surrounding areas to access a range of Hazelden substance abuse services. At Hazelden Chicago, people can receive a comprehensive assessment of their chemical health needs and then access the appropriate components of the Hazelden continuum. They may receive services at Hazelden Chicago, or they may be referred to primary residential treatment offered in Center City or another Hazelden site. It remains to be seen whether Chicago will increase primary referrals to Center City. This had been the intent at New York, but managed care and a shortened primary program effectively prevented that from happening.

Hazelden Chicago

Complementing the inpatient and outpatient services in Chicago is a range of professional services that address the mental health and living skills of each patient. An outpatient center for young people opened in 1998. Hazelden Chicago is expected to become a tremendous source of education and fellowship. A bookstore carrying the range of books, tapes, workbooks, and pamphlets distributed by Hazelden Publishing is housed at Hazelden Chicago. Addiction training for professionals, workshops for recovering people, and alumni outreach events are also held at the center.

The Lessons of History

From its first three expansion ventures—New Pioneer House, Hanley-Hazelden, and the New York Fellowship Club—Hazelden experienced numerous growing pains. It took awhile for Center City to understand that too much centralized control created an unhealthy environment with paternalistic and ineffective leadership. Once Center City experienced the benefits of tapping the local community for managerial and clinical leadership and learned to balance decision making and accountability with local boards, the foundation had discovered the synergy that can occur between a centralized senior management and a committed local community. Only then can a strong team working together for the common good emerge.

Chicago seems to have learned from these experiences. Center City contributed bridge money, selected experienced leadership from the talented pool of people in Chicago, and has a workable governance structure in place. Florida, New York, and Chicago have all been adept and enthusiastic about fundraising, which has been an essential source of revenue for the three centers.

What else has Hazelden and its regional operations yet to learn from these excursions abroad besides the need to blend cultures, to center the project within the community, to select appropriate and experienced staff, and to make allowances for mistakes? Hazelden would do well to take a lesson from the dependent people it treats so expertly—the lessons of powerlessness and surrendering control.

In the last analysis, success derives not so much from a blending of cultures as from bridling the urge to have complete control on the part of both Hazelden and its satellite boards. Both need an injection of humility. The history of the past fifteen years should allow for a greater decentralization on the part of Center City. Beyond safe-guarding the philosophy and the general goals of the Hazelden model, new ventures ought to be allowed more freedom and independence in the development and evolution of their own programs. Satellite boards and their outspoken members need to practice the humility of the recovering person, understand the nature of crisis as it applies to institutions and boards, and not panic unnecessarily. More easily said than done for both sides in Hazelden's past new ventures.

Every once in a while all the parties concerned need to call time out and reflect upon the nature of a spiritual awakening: I cannot do it by myself; I need others to help me. It is the "we" of the program, not the "I," that has carried Hazelden and its partners forward for the past fifty years, and, God willing, will guarantee another fifty.

Reflections on . . .
"There Is a Flower Before You."

There is a flower before you
to represent each day
I spent at Hazelden Chicago.

The flower is a symbol
of more beauty and wonder
than my mind can fathom.

Hazelden is a symbol
of more kindness, well-being, and joyous uplifting
than my mind has ever known.

As each gracious petal
withers and falls away,
may a stirring in your heart
be a reminder of the miracle of the life
each of you shares with another.

Though my journey
with God's grace is new,
the only thing I can now do for you,
with love, strength, and hope from thee,
is to set the soul of another free.

ANONYMOUS PATIENT

Walking trail on the Hazelden Center City campus

6

The Redemptive Journey

THE CLOSING IN 1992 of the Clinical Pastoral Education Program (CPE), which trained clergy of all denominations how to minister to clients with an alcohol or drug problem, was a sad event in Hazelden's history. Without knowing why the program was closed, the program alumni were hurt and angered by its demise. For many of them, the program defined the spiritual character of Hazelden, and its end signaled the loss of Hazelden's original soul. The pain that they experienced blinded them to the fact that the Pastoral Department and its clergy (not the same as the CPE program and its trainees) maintained a very important role as part of the multidisciplinary team that served the patients.

Less tumultuous and less visible to the alumni was the loss of the meditation rooms to the encroaching needs of support staff. As one longtime employee remarked, these rooms stood as visible symbols of the spiritual dimension of Hazelden's program and its commitment to the steps of AA. The history of Hazelden is an illustrative chapter in the ongoing history of the spirituality of AA. And even though the Hazelden program is not the AA program per se, it is inextricably interwoven with AA principles and practice. Hazelden would not be Hazelden if it dissociated itself from the spirituality of AA and its Steps.

Hazelden's mission is the restoration of the self-worth, dignity, and humanity of each and every individual who seeks its help. This

107

is synonymous with the restoration and renewal of a person's spirituality. For to be truly human is to be truly spiritual; to be truly spiritual is to be truly human. Because chemical dependency is a spiritual illness, it requires a spiritual remedy. The Twelfth Step of AA speaks of a spiritual awakening. Hazelden's intimate association with AA weds it to the concept and reality of a spiritual awakening. Although it may be risky and audacious to associate Hazelden's success with a purpose so seemingly vague as a spiritual awakening, this association as an indicator of success merits consideration.

What is it that AA has captured and Hazelden is successful in replicating about the human condition and spirituality that speaks not only to recovering people but also to humanity at large? Spirituality encompasses the issues of dualism, that is, of the two selves vying for dominance within a person, of dying and rising, of encounters with mortality, of redemptive healing journeys, of the phenomenology of crisis and the power and practice of discernment. Spirituality is also illustrated through the principles and ascetical practices contained in the Twelve Steps.

The following poem highlights a human condition common to all of us:

> *Within my earthly temple there's a crowd,*
> *There's one of us that's humble, one that's proud,*
> *There's one that's brokenhearted for his sins,*
> *There's one that unrepentant sits and grins,*
> *There's one that loves his neighbor as himself,*
> *and one that cares for naught but fame and self;*
> *From much corroding care I should be free,*
> *If I could once determine which is me.*
> ("My Name is Legion," from *Masterpieces of Religious Verse*)

The passage describes a condition that has played a prominent role in the history of Western thought and spirituality. It is the theme of the dualism that exists in men and women and that can assume many forms and roles: the two selves within us; the two paths that lead in different directions; the struggle between light and darkness, between good and evil, between the spirit and the flesh, between sin and grace, between this world and a transcendent one. Poets, religious thinkers, writers, psychiatrists, people from sundry fields have all sought to explain the origins of dualism, its personal drama, and its consequences. Two men, two thousand years apart, representing two diverse professions, described dualism in very different language but with essentially the same content. Paul of Tarsus caught the attention of his and subsequent generations when he wrote in the first century A.D. his letter to the Romans describing the enigma that man sees in himself as a desperate situation derived from a conflict in his inmost depths. It is the cleavage between his dominating desire and his actual performance: "I do not do what I want to—and what I do I detest. Miserable man that I am. Who will save me from the body of this death?"

This vacillation between the two selves has also concerned psychologists. In the twentieth century, the famous Swiss psychiatrist Carl Jung comprehended and analyzed this dualism in a unique manner. Like Paul of Tarsus, Jung demonstrated some incisive insights into human nature when he wrote, "What drives people to war with themselves is the intuition or knowledge that they consist of two people in opposition to one another. The conflict may be between the sensual and the spiritual man, or between the ego and the shadow. It is what Faust means when he says: 'Two souls, alas, dwell within my breast apart.'"

What some call the social self, Jung calls the *persona,* the part of ourselves we see fit to disclose to others: "It is like an outer garment in which we cloak ourselves as we present ourselves to the world. It helps us to develop a particular style, facilitates the task of living, and renders us socially acceptable. It is not necessarily a false aspect of oneself, but it is certainly not the whole truth about oneself."

Now the underside of the persona is the *shadow.* The shadow is the unconscious, lying beneath the surface, containing the hidden, repressed, and unfavorable aspect of the personality. "Whatever seems unacceptable to our persona we try to banish from our lives. But what we have banished never really leaves. And if we do not own these unacceptable impulses or characteristics, they tend to own us. The shadow is never more dangerous than when the conscious personality has lost touch with it."

All of us are called to grow in consciousness, honesty, and

courage and to struggle with the duality in us, living with that inherent tension. Our personal experience allows us to identify with the sentiments of the poem quoted previously:

> *Within my earthly temple there's a crowd,*
> *There's one of us that's humble, one that's proud.*

It is not difficult to see in the addiction and recovery process the conflict between the two selves. The addictive process can be described as a struggle between the true self and the addicted self. Recovering people have experienced this dualism in an initially degrading but ultimately rewarding fashion. (Craig Nakken's book *The Addictive Personality* has been the source for my analogy.)

In the beginning the struggle between the two selves is a private, internal one. The true self senses that the addictive self is starting to emerge and begins to fight it with its own willpower. It loses these small struggles, feels guilty and shameful. With each defeat the true self quickly and sorrowfully promises to do better, to control the use of the chemicals. But the cycle becomes painfully repetitive. Preoccupation with the struggle and the loss of control dominate the thinking of the true self. This initial stage is an internal and private one because the true self has a "no talk" rule. It is not about to talk the problem over with others. The true self believes it can manage the problem without any help. In reality it is ashamed to talk about the problem with others. Consequently, whenever stressed, the true self turns more and more to chemicals for relief.

The second stage of this addictive process emerges when the addicted self, much to the horror, consternation, and shame of the true self, goes public. The addiction process has moved from the internal to the external world. The true self is no longer in control; the true self and the addicted self change places. The addicted self has given the coup de grace to the real self. When asked about his or her behavior, the constant refrain is, "Well, what's it to you?" The addicted self terrorizes family and friends. They can never be certain which self will make an appearance at the family table or the social event.

Finally, in the last stage, the addictive process has worked so well that the true self literally begins to break down. The addiction has created so much stress and so much pain that the self's coping and relating skills totally collapse. The addictive self cares nothing about

110

true self and nothing about anybody else. The true self literally does not know how to connect with people anymore. It is also painfully clear that in this third stage of addiction the chemical no longer provides relief. For some, suicide becomes a haunting specter. When that path is not taken, what remains is just as frightening. The true self is doomed to isolation. The spirit has been lost, as has the will to live and to connect with other people. For all practical purposes the true self is dying. It is preeminently an encounter with one's mortality.

What has occurred during this process? In each stage of this process the addicted self has destroyed relationships, has abandoned intimacy in favor of intensity with a chemical. The addicted self has moved from the land of the living to the surreal landscape of objects. This is a major spiritual issue—the abandonment of people and relationships for material things. The individual finds oneself in a wild, tumbling, hopeless freefall, which can only end when one is willing to surrender to one's powerlessness, thereby killing the addicted self.

We can compare this addictive process, this encounter with one's mortality, with the phenomenon of human crisis. Everyone encounters crises which are decisive and sacred moments in one's odyssey through life. (Although it may be difficult to see the alcoholic's despair as something sacred, it truly is.) A crisis contains an element of ambiguity and the person undergoing it does not know what will be decided. The negative side of the crisis evokes confusion and disorientation, which can come on suddenly, even abruptly, or it can emerge gradually and subtly. The person's normal way of seeing his or her identity begins to break down. The customary way of acting begins to crumble. The process is trying to tell that person that something has to be reorganized. It is a warning signal that an effort must be made to establish another method or approach to life. In a real sense, a person experiences some part of themselves as dying. It can also be described as an emptying process.

The positive dimension of the crisis rests in the conscious awareness that, indeed, this disorientation is a very normal aspect of growth. God, or one's Higher Power, seeks through a crisis (or a sacred time) to draw us out of a controlled situation, and from the potency of the disruption, disorder, even chaos, the positive new attitude and behavior will erupt or emerge (the amount of pain will determine the verb used). The rebirth, the renaissance, the rising follows from the dying, or the emptying. In that sense, every crisis is an analogous encounter with one's own mortality. Crisis is simply the way that humans grow, running counter to the myth that growth occurs in smooth even steps in our journey. In a sense, every crisis is a dress rehearsal. If one hasn't rehearsed well, that person will go kicking and screaming into death.

In the case of the chemically dependent person, we have already seen the negative elements of the crisis, the confusion, the disorientation, the breakdown of the person's normal way of acting. If addiction is a downward spiral with the breakdown of relationships, then recovery is an upward spiral re-establishing the relationships that have been broken. It is a reordering of priorities. Recovery for addicted people begins the moment they splinter the beam of their denial and commence to understand the life-threatening nature of their illness. This encounter with one's mortality is ultimately spiritual as it archetypally involves a death-rising process—a dying to the addicted self and a rising of the real self. The encounter can be none other than spiritual as recovering people ponder their flirtation with death (of the real self) and their answers to the questions, "Who am I?" and "Will I make a difference?" It is the search for ultimate meaning. As Bill Wilson, the cofounder of AA, wrote in *Pass It On*, "More than most people, I think, alcoholics want to know who they are, what life is all about, whether they have a divine origin, an appointed destiny, and whether there is a system of cosmic justice and love."

Recovery is a journey intersected by life experiences that will continue to provoke crises and evoke change. Crises are an essential part of that journey and transform it into a spiritual one. They are constant reminders of our ultimate encounter with mortality. As crises help us change and grow, we ultimately discover the whole persons that we are meant and challenged to be.

Bill Wilson recognized the similarity in his own thinking and in that of Carl Jung. In fact, Wilson wrote to Jung in January 1961 thanking him for reinforcing AA's belief that alcoholism was a hopeless condition that would not respond to medical or psychiatric treatment. What was needed, Jung believed, was a radical conversion—a spiritual or religious experience. Bill wrote that this was the foundation upon which AA had been built.

Obviously, it would be inappropriate to derive from the brief cor-

Bill W., cofounder of Alcoholics Anonymous, wrote, "More than most people, I think alcoholics want to know who they are, what life is all about, whether they have a divine origin, an appointed destiny, and whether there is a system of cosmic justice and love."

respondence a causal relationship, or for that matter any relationship whatsoever, between AA and Jung's psychology except for the common belief in and view of the human condition shared by a broad spectrum of philosophers, psychologists, and theologians—a belief that it stands in need of healing. Nonetheless there are some surprising similarities between the two.

Essentially, Jung described alcoholism as a spiritual illness at the basis of which is humankind's yearning for wholeness. Jung described the journey toward wholeness as an individuation process. That process entails a struggle that is accomplished in stages and is a work of self-redemption that will make the person a whole and undivided personality—an individual.

In this sense the path, the journey, the process of individuation, according to Jung, can be called a *heilsweg*—in the twofold meaning of the German word, a way of healing and a way of salvation. The heilsweg, the healing journey, demands revolution, the overthrow of the existing order, inner division, and renewal. "Individual self-reflection, return of the individual to the ground of human nature, and to his own deepest being, with its individual and social destiny, here is the beginning of a cure for that blindness which reigns at the present hour." (*Psychological Reflections.* J. Jacobi and R. F. Huff, editors, p. 230).

While the Jungian heilsweg is predicated on the ego's struggle with the personal and collective unconscious, it mirrors very well everyone's personal encounter with crisis and, in a very special way, what I like to call the alcoholic's encounter with mortality. Whether we use the analogy of heilsweg or of life as a journey highlighted by crises, both contain the metaphor of dying and rising particularly applicable to the odyssey of the chemically dependent person.

The major obstacle for chemically dependent people is that they seek to cut the journey short, to bypass or leap beyond the demands of the individuation process. They seek to become whole not through struggle and self-examination, not through the reconciliation of opposites or tensions, and especially not through the experience of pain brought about by the death and rising of crisis situations that life demands of all of us. Rather dependent people seek to become whole, to complete the opus as Jung would entitle it, without walking the heilsweg—the healing/redemptive march. It is in this sense that alcoholism is but a symptom of the most comprehensive *dis-ease* (discomfort), namely, humankind's search for self, for meaning, for wholeness.

In this context, Bill W. composed the Twelve Steps as the remedy for humankind's dis-ease. The Big Book becomes the heilsweg manual, mapping out the healing journey and providing a set of spiritual exercises—the Twelve Steps—to accompany recovering people on their spiritual odyssey, of especial importance for those critical encounters with their own mortality that will occur throughout life's journey. Like spring meltwaters cascading through a canyon, the Twelve Steps unleash a tremendous healing/redemptive power. (The word *redemption* frightens some people as being too theological, too religious, smacking as it does of practices that make recovering people uneasy. But if one can get past that original anxiety and consider what the word really means, namely, healing or mending, then it can become more appealing.) For who on this planet does not feel the need for healing, for dealing with that incompleteness, that lack of wholeness, that vulnerability that lies deep within us—a shadow from which we would like to flee but which lurks behind us no matter which way we turn? At their root, all the great religious traditions stress the healing presence of God, Yahweh, Allah.

114

Hazelden and the Redemptive Journey

In the course of its history, Hazelden has taken the initiative in a variety of ways to demonstrate its ongoing commitment to recovering people on their redemptive journey. (Because it was ongoing and continuous, the name Recovery Services rather than Rehabilitation Services seemed more appropriate to describe this mission.) As a result Hazelden has developed a continuum of recovery services to assist people on their recovery journeys. The primary units, the Renewal Center and the Center for Ongoing Recovery, serve recovering people in their ongoing encounters with mortality. This healing power permeates the hallowed halls of Hazelden. That is why it is a sacred place, a place of healing.

In offering residential primary services, Hazelden hopes to assist recovering people in their initial and radical encounter with mortality. This initiation into the redemptive journey has been ritualized by the graduation ceremonies from the primary units. Still, the peril of relapse and the danger of stunted spiritual growth—during subsequent encounters with mortality—are very real.

When people first come to Hazelden for primary care, Hazelden provides the experience of a caring community, a place where one can feel safe (saved), an environment of comfort and compassion. No wonder that M. Scott Peck (psychiatrist, spiritual writer, and author of *The Road Less Traveled*) calls the AA self-help movement one of the three great spiritual phenomena of the twentieth century (along with the Holocaust and the Second Vatican Council). The particular reason for its greatness, according to Peck, is that the paradigm of community it developed was exactly what this atomized and unredeemed twentieth century needed.

Besides being a community of caring individuals who are there when needed, Hazelden, modeled upon the AA fellowship, is at a deeper level a healing community. All of us stand in need of healing, although many would like to believe and act as if they stand in need of nothing. Most eventually find the appeal of rugged individualism to be an empty or deceptive delusion. Despite the nineteenth and twentieth centuries' proud boast that science would eradicate the last vestiges of original sin and erase the need for religion that promised consolation and healing, the four Apocalyptic horsemen still roam at will.

The chemically dependent person searching for recovery understands and experiences more than most the need for healing. At Hazelden this healing comes about through the fellowship on the unit. There the redemptive act is most evident when one member graces another by sharing—those small, often overlooked acts of listening and speaking. One of the meanings of *grace* is a gift of God. Therein lies the redemptive power. When a personal story of weakness or strength is shared, it creates the opportunity to identify with another human being. It is the beginning of the heilsweg. Put another way: "Sharing one's story with another human being is sacred ground." Through the healing community on a Hazelden unit, individual members gain great redemptive power.

Indeed, this presents a striking contrast to most churches in which redemption is supposed to prevail. In the AA Fellowship, "Everybody opens up about their brokenness and their failures, and they heal. . . . What happens in churches is just the opposite. . . . We sit there with our pain and brokenness, and we never share it and we don't heal. Our churches are just the opposite of a healing community. . . . We have to work hard toward becoming the kind of community where it is safe to tell your story." ("An Interview with Dave Hilton, M.D.: Global Health and the Limits of Medicine," *Second Opinion*, January 1993, p. 58.) Hazelden moves people from communities of pretense to healing communities.

But encounters with mortality do not end after graduation from Hazelden. Crisis is a constant, whether it appears in the form of a danger of relapse or another form. It is an essential part of the human experience. Hazelden's commitment to the recovering person's continuing journey was reinforced by the creation of the Renewal Center in 1984, a safe haven where individuals could re-encounter their mortality. Capturing the serenity of the Old Lodge, it is a place where one can again engage in dialogue with oneself, with others, and with a Higher Power to avoid the ever-present temptation to fall back into self-alienation, social isolation, and spiritual emptiness.

Adjacent to the ground on which the Renewal Center was constructed was a legendary burial ground. According to the unwritten

116

anecdotal history related by the old-timers of Hazelden, the hill with its neat rows of planted trees that one sees directly out the windows of the dining hall was called Resentment Hill. It used to be pock-marked with little mounds that resembled gopher hills. The story goes that all those little hills were raised by patients who upon the completion of the Fifth Step were told to dig a hole on the slope and bury their resentments. Apocryphal or not, it is a fitting meditation for those who return to the Renewal Center to examine and divest themselves of whatever obstacles are standing in the way of their personal redemptive journey, their journey to wholeness.

The idea for the Renewal Center was cultivated and cherished by Dan Anderson, who hoped that it would be established before he retired. (Had Anderson not demurred strongly, Pat Butler would have named it the Anderson Center.) The alumni and other friends of Hazelden regarded the concept so highly that they donated the $2 million needed to build and furnish it. Figuratively, Anderson envisioned the recovery journey as commencing in the Old Lodge, the original site for Rehabilitation Services, and continuing in the Renewal Center. But unlike Rehabilitation, the Renewal Center would not be a part of the health delivery system, with its plethora of rules and regulations. There would be a return to simplicity: of admission, expectations, and price. Simplicity, spirit, service, and singularity of purpose! In a certain sense the Renewal Center also recaptured the serenity and solitude that surrounded the Old Lodge, an ambiance that gradually evaporated during the decades of expansion.

Reflections on . . .
"The Renewal Center— A Vital Part of My Recovery Program"

I went through treatment at Hazelden in 1971. After twenty years of sobriety, however, I had a relapse—a big one. I contacted Hazelden for help and ended up participating in their Relapse Prevention Program. Thanks to it, I was able to identify the subtle and not-too-subtle triggers in my life that caused my relapse. It gave me what I needed to monitor my behaviors to prevent another relapse.

A view from the top of Resentment Hill, looking toward the Renewal Center

One of the keys for me is staying active in the program. Coming to the Renewal Center for the experiences there are a vital part of my recovery program. The facility is wonderful, and the seminars, workshops, and meetings are outstanding.

I find that the Renewal Center is a quiet place to come home to. It's a temporary safe place, a respite. It's a place where I can step back, get off of life's freeway for several days, and take a look at things. I look for rest and reevaluation there. It gives me an opportunity to refocus and to take a look at where I've been, where I'm at, and where I need to be. It's also a place I can go when certain sobriety-threatening situations start to develop—a place where I can get a "checkup" before anything gets out of hand. After my time there, I can come back to my daily life, feeling more calm and confident, and renewed. We say in the program, "Read the Big Book, go to meetings, and don't drink!"

118

I'd like to add one more: "Go to the Renewal Center at Hazelden if you can!"

DAVE O.

To this day, I still go back at least twice a year to the Renewal Center at Hazelden for the lectures and to give myself the time to reflect. It helps remind me of where I was, what I was like, and how far I've come. I never want to lose that feeling.

DENISE Mc.

The Renewal Center was envisioned as a response to the ongoing needs of the recovery community, as a harbor where individuals could reflect, nourish, and strengthen themselves for their continuing journey. The death-rising encountered in primary treatment would have to be replicated in a variety of ways if growth and change were to continue. The Renewal Center was intended to assist in the resolution of those subsequent encounters. No one would have to go it alone. Our journey through life is a community affair—someone has to say, "I will be with you." Hazelden said it with the Renewal Center. As one of the center's many grateful alumni observed, "The Renewal Center is like the AA program. From the front the building seems small, with a narrow opening. When you get inside, however, you see how large and comfortable it really is. When you go all the way through and look back upon it—it seems awesome."

Indeed, the Renewal Center is symbolic of the art, ritual, and practice of discernment, especially at the time of crisis. It is the Eleventh Step incarnated: "Sought through prayer and meditation to improve our conscious contact with God *as we understand Him,* praying only for knowledge of His will for us and the power to carry that out."

A major reason for the success of the recovery process is that the AA program demands continuous and uninterrupted scrutiny of oneself, so that the latent possibilities of betrayal by the shadow, or the false self, will not emerge to sidetrack the traveler from the path to wholeness. "To thine own self be true," contains perennial wisdom and value—it is the pearl of great price. But only the ascetical discipline of self-knowledge and self-discovery will allow us to mirror our own real selves, which we can own and to which we can be true.

A decade after building the Renewal Center, Hazelden took its third major step to assist recovering people on their redemptive journey—it established the Center for Ongoing Recovery. The new center both incorporates and extends the mission of the Renewal Center. Essentially, the Center for Ongoing Recovery (COR, which in Latin means "heart") was intended as a reservoir of multiple resources for the recovery community. It was to be a multidimensional center to respond both to the lingering and associated effects of chemical dependency as well as to nonrelated issues of emotional, social, spiritual, and physical well-being.

Often a patient leaves Hazelden free of chemicals but not necessarily free of other related or unrelated problems. While it is true

*Inside the
Renewal Center*

that much of the crazy behavior associated with the use of chemicals does go away once the drinking or using ceases, it is also true that some unrelated dysfunction may remain, such as depression, spiritual inertia, or social misbehavior. Hazelden's commitment is to the healing of the whole person. The healing journey has multiple bends, curves, dead ends, road blocks, and one-way streets. Hazelden seeks to provide guidance through what often seems to be a labyrinthian maze, always remaining faithful to its principles of abstinence, behavioral change, and the wisdom encompassed in the Twelve Steps.

Hazelden's recovery programs are successful because they neither compromise the AA process and its spirituality nor cater to those who overlook, ridicule, or simply do not understand AA. I have referred to Hazelden as a graceful place, full of gracious people. The act of one person talking to another is a gracious act. The formula for recovery is that people are gracious. Hazelden's survival depends upon its ability to assist recovering people in doing just that at whatever stage of their redemptive journey they may be at.

Outside the back of the Renewal Center

As this book goes to press, an architectural firm has completed plans for a new meditation center to be built on the site of the Old Lodge. It will be more than an adequate substitute for the meditation rooms sequestered by ancillary staff, a visible symbol of the spiritual dimension of Hazelden's unique services to the recovery community. It will serve as a spiritual wayside—a resting place for patients, staff, alumni, and visitors who feel the need to take time out, to be quiet, to look deeply within themselves.

All of us need to get away, to shut out the many distractions that engulf us in this modern world. A serious problem for our society today is that it is so heavily into glitz and glitter and the panoply of the external and the superficial that it pays little attention and even less heed to what stirs deep within us. Most of us are distracted, reluctant, and frightened to ponder the deeper realities of our lives.

There is so much noise that we cannot hear our interior voices and the rumors of angels. Our minds are racing and so cluttered it is difficult to be still and reflect on what groans within us.

We are filled with so much information it is impossible to contemplate about the one thing necessary.

We are so preoccupied with the artificial and the frivolous that the lilies of the field and the birds of the air are a distraction and their meaning lost upon us.

There is so much greed that a life of detachment cannot be imagined much less realized and lived.

There is so much envy and resentment that the sentiments that ennoble us lay untouched and unclaimed.

These and a thousand and one other distractions prevent us from searching our souls, from hearing the gentle lapping of the waters that purify us, or the soft whisperings from deep within that beckon us like a compass needle to the real issues that must be dealt with if we are to make any progress on our redemptive journey or in the realm of the spirit.

Bibliographical Essay

The principal sources for this little volume are my own recollections supported by

- Interviews with past and present Hazelden board members and staff
- Minutes and agendas from Hazelden board meetings in Center City (1975–1998), at Hanley-Hazelden at St. Mary's (1985–1995), and at the Center for Youth and Families
- Harold Swift's correspondence with Pat Butler (1976–1988)
- The Richard Byrd Report (1983)
- Various collections of minutes (president's team, total quality management, Rehabilitation Division meetings)
- Hazelden newsletters (both internal and external)

While these reflections deal with history, not every available source has been utilized. Moreover, not every source that has been used has been historically tested, particularly the numerous private interviews where time and bias have taken their toll on personal memories and recollections.

The only footnote to this volume is this: It is only recently that the Hazelden Pittman Archives, a relative newcomer to Hazelden's services, has made a determined effort to collect and preserve materials related to the history of alcoholism and Hazelden's history.

APPENDIX A

Hazelden's Chronology of Important Events

1949   Hazelden incorporated, January 10.
First patient, April.
Official opening, May.

1952   Pat Butler, president of Hazelden.

1953   Fellowship Club, halfway house for men, opened in St. Paul.

1954   Publication of *Twenty-Four Hours a Day.* Informal beginning of Hazelden Publishing Services.

1956   Dia Linn, residential program for women, opened in Dellwood, Minnesota.

1963   Informal counselor training program initiated.

1964–1966   Expansion of residential program at Center City—Ignatia Hall and four new units: Tiebout, Silkworth, Dia Linn, and Shoemaker.

1966   Initiation of Clinical Pastoral Education Program.

1969–1970   Further expansion at Center City: Bigelow Auditorium and Lilly and Jellinek Halls.

1972   Beginning of Family Program and Professional In Residence Program (teachers).

1974   Butler building constructed.
Accreditation by the Joint Commission on the Accreditation of Hospitals.

1975   Alumni Association established.

1976   Beginning of outpatient programs (St. Paul).

1977   Completion of Cronin Hall for patients,
        Family Program, and training.

1978   Publication of *Not-God*—history of Alcoholics Anony-
        mous.

1979   Opening of Nicollet Resource Center—Minneapolis.

1980   Construction of maintenance facilities and expansion
        of Butler building.
        Publication of *Food for Thought.*

1981   Purchase of Pioneer House to serve the adolescent and
        young adult.
        Women's outpatient program established at
        Nicollet Clinic.
        Initiation of Hazelden prevention programs.

1982   Clarence Snyder Hall, a halfway house for
        adolescents in Wisconsin, opened.
        Publication of *Each Day a New Beginning.*

1983   Hanley-Hazelden (Florida) Resource Clinic opened.

1984   Renewal Center opened.

1985   Purchase of Park Avenue facility to serve as
        Minneapolis Resource Center and future home
        of Hazelden Services Inc.
        Bradley Hall, a Wisconsin residence for adolescents,
        opened.
        Cork Center, a resource center for Health Promotion
        and Training, opened.
        Richmond Walker, publishing headquarters, opened.

1986   Dan Anderson retires. Harold Swift, new president.
        Hanley-Hazelden Residential Program opened.

1987   Texas Southwest Region Resource Center opened.
        Codependent No More published.

1988   Demolition of Old Lodge.
        Hazelden Services Incorporated formed,
        residing at Park Avenue.
        Hazelden Education Services Incorporated formed in
        Ireland (later named Hazelden, Ireland).

1991   Hazelden Information Center established.

1992   New York Fellowship Club opened.

Chicago Resource Center established.
Hazelden Institute established for public policy
and research and learning.
Jerry Spicer succeeds Harry Swift as president
of Hazelden.

1993 Counseling Clinic licensed at the Hazelden Center
for Youth and Families.
Pittman Archives for History of Alcoholism
established on Center City campus.

1996 Hazelden web site established on Internet.

1997 Hazelden Chicago Residential Facility opened.
Women's Recovery Community established in
New Brighton, Minnesota.

1998 New Hazelden Mission Statement:

*Hazelden will help build recovery in the lives of
individuals, families, and communities affected by
alcoholism, drug dependency, and related diseases.*

APPENDIX B

*The Twelve Steps of Alcoholics Anonymous**

1. We admitted we were powerless over alcohol—that our lives had become unmanageable.
2. Came to believe that a Power greater than ourselves could restore us to sanity.
3. Made a decision to turn our will and our lives over to the care of God *as we understood Him.*
4. Made a searching and fearless moral inventory of ourselves.
5. Admitted to God, to ourselves, and to another human being the exact nature of our wrongs.
6. Were entirely ready to have God remove all these defects of character.
7. Humbly asked Him to remove our shortcomings.
8. Made a list of all persons we had harmed, and became willing to make amends to them all.
9. Made direct amends to such people wherever possible, except when to do so would injure them or others.
10. Continued to take personal inventory and when we were wrong promptly admitted it.
11. Sought through prayer and meditation to improve our conscious contact with God *as we understood Him,* praying only for knowledge of His will for us and the power to carry that out.
12. Having had a spiritual awakening as the result of these steps, we tried to carry this message to alcoholics, and to practice these principles in all our affairs.

* The Twelve Steps of AA are taken from *Alcoholics Anonymous*, 3d ed., published by AA World Services, Inc., New York, N.Y., 59–60. Reprinted with permission of AA World Services, Inc. (See editor's note on copyright page.) 129

Index

ABOUT THE AUTHOR

DAMIAN MCELRATH, PH.D., served in a variety of positions at Hazelden from 1978 until his retirement in 1995, most notably as executive vice president of Recovery Services. McElrath came to Hazelden after twenty years of teaching, counseling, and administrative work; he was president of St. Bonaventure University from 1972 to 1976. He is well known for his lectures on addiction, spirituality and the Twelve Steps and has lectured at the Rutgers Summer School of Alcohol Studies and its European branch from 1981 to 1998. He has published numerous scholarly books and articles on historical and theological topics and is the author of the Hazelden books *Hazelden: A Spiritual Odyssey* (1987), *Dan Anderson: A Biography* (1999), and *Patrick Butler: A Biography* (1999).